Radical Hope

# Radical Hope

## ETHICS IN THE FACE OF

## CULTURAL DEVASTATION

JONATHAN LEAR

HARVARD UNIVERSITY PRESS

Cambridge, Massachusetts, and London, England

2006

Publication of this book has been supported through the generous provisions of the
Maurice and Lula Bradley Smith Memorial Fund.

*Library of Congress Cataloging-in-Publication Data*
Lear, Jonathan.
Radical hope : ethics in the face of cultural devastation / Jonathan Lear.
p.   cm.
Includes bibliographical references (p.  ) and index.
ISBN-13: 978-0-674-02329-1 (alk. paper)
ISBN-10: 0-674-02329-3
1. Ethics.   2. Social change.   3. Social sciences and ethics.
4. Crow Indians—Social life and customs.   I. Title.

BJ52.L43 2006
70—dc21        2006043484

*For Gabriel*

# Contents

# Illustrations

Radical Hope

# I

## AFTER THIS, NOTHING HAPPENED

### *A Peculiar Vulnerability*

SHORTLY BEFORE HE DIED, Plenty Coups, the last great chief of the Crow nation, reached out across the "clash of civilizations" and told his story to a white man. Frank B. Linderman had come to Montana in 1885 as a teenager, and he became a trapper, hunter, and cowboy. He lived in a cabin in the woods near Flathead Lake and was intimately associated with the Crows. From the book he wrote, recounting Plenty Coups's story, it is clear that he and Plenty Coups had become friends. "I am glad I have told you these things, Sign-talker," Plenty Coups says at the end of the book. "You have felt my heart, and I have felt yours. I know you will tell only what I have said, that your writing will be straight like your tongue, and I will sign your paper with my thumb, so that your people and mine will know I told you the things you have written down."[1] It is a marvelous account of the exploits of a young man growing up at a time when the Crow were still a vibrant tribe of nomadic hunters. Even so, Linderman is reticent about how well he has got to know his subject. In the foreword he says, "I am convinced that no white man has ever thoroughly known the Indian, and such a work as this must suffer because of the widely different views of life held by the two races, red and white. I have studied the Indian for more than forty years, not coldly, but with sympathy; yet even now I do not feel that I know much about him. He has told me many times that I *do* know him—that I have 'felt his heart,' but whether this is so I am not certain."[2]

But the words that haunt me are not part of Plenty Coups's story, though they do come from his mouth. In an author's note at the end of the book, Linderman says that he was unable to get Plenty Coups to talk about anything that had happened after the Crow were confined to a reservation:

> Plenty Coups refused to speak of his life after the passing of the buffalo, so that his story seems to have been broken off, leaving many years unaccounted for. "I have not told you half of what happened when I was young," he said, when urged to go on. "I can think back and tell you much more of war and horse-stealing. But when the buffalo went away the hearts of my people fell to the ground, and they could not lift them up again. After this nothing happened. There was little singing anywhere. Besides," he added sorrowfully, "you know that part of my life as well as I do. You saw what happened to us when the buffalo went away."[3]

*After this nothing happened:* what could Plenty Coups's utterance mean? If we take him at his word, he seems to be saying that there was an event or a happening—the buffalo's going away—something Plenty Coups can refer to as a "this," such that after *this,* there are no more happenings. Or, to get the temporality correct, Plenty Coups came to see, as he looked back, that there was a moment such that after this, nothing happen*ed*. It would seem to be the retrospective declaration of a moment when history came to an end. But what could it mean for history to exhaust itself?

The question is so odd that there is a natural inclination to interpret Plenty Coups as saying something that makes more immediate sense to us. One possibility is to focus on Plenty Coups's claim that after the buffalo went away, "the hearts of my people fell to the ground and they could not lift them up again." As he puts it, "there was little singing anywhere." This might suggest a psychological interpretation: after the buffalo went away, after they were confined to a reservation, the Crow people became depressed; things ceased to matter to them. It was for them *as though* nothing happened. This psychological interpretation is given added support by the author's account of Plenty Coups adding *sorrowfully*, "Besides, you know that part of my life as well as I do." In general, it is an astonishing claim for anyone to say that another person knows a part of his adult life as well as he himself does. Although we may be corrected in various ways by others, we take ourselves to have authority when it comes to the narratives of our own lives. Plenty Coups seems to be abdicating this authority when it comes to this period. Indeed, he seems to suggest that *anyone*—not just the author—who saw what happened when the buffalo went away would be competent to tell that part of his life as well as he could. That is, any competent third-person observer would know all there was to know. This suggests that, according to Plenty Coups, there is no importantly first-person narrative to tell of this period. It is as though there is no longer an I there.

This strange thought is made sense of by saying: Plenty Coups is depressed—or he is giving voice to the depression that engulfed his tribe.

This interpretation has the merit of making sense. And it is plausible: Plenty Coups might have been giving voice to a malaise that infected his tribe. The interpretation thus fits what philosophers call the principle of humanity: that we should try to interpret others as saying something true—guided by our own sense of what is true and of what they could reasonably believe.[4] But note, we have gained plausibility in interpretation by changing the subject matter. Ostensibly Plenty Coups is making a claim about the world: that after a certain point nothing happened. We have interpreted him as saying something true by taking him to be expressing something about his psyche, and the psyches of his fellow Crow tribesmen. This may fit the *principle* of humanity, but there is a question of whether it fits *Plenty Coups's* humanity. Might he not be giving utterance to a darker thought, one that is more difficult for us to understand? If so, then the psychological interpretation is in too much of a rush. If he is talking about the Crow people becoming depressed, we can understand him in a minute and move on. But if he is talking about happenings coming to an end . . . ; how can we interpret him as saying something true?

Certainly there is evidence to suggest that Plenty Coups was not depressed—and thus that we ought to interpret him in some other way. When we consider the rest of his life, it is extraordinary how active Plenty Coups was. And while it is true that some depressed people can keep busy—as a way of warding off the experience of depression—there was a kind of enthusiasm in Plenty Coups's activity that belies this interpretation. He avidly took up farming life and urged other members of the tribe to do so. With apparent pride, he displayed his crops at agricultural shows and won prizes. He was active in bringing the other Crow chiefs together to form a united front in negotiating with the U.S. government. As a young leader he traveled to Washington, D.C., as the head of a Crow delegation that successfully lobbied to prevent a bill that would appropriate more Crow land from coming to the Senate floor.[5] This was the first of several trips he made to Washington, defending the rights of the Crow. Plenty Coups visited George Washington's house at Mt. Vernon and became fascinated with the idea of donating his own home to the nation. It is now a state park in Montana. And in 1921, at the national ceremony to establish the Tomb of the Unknown Soldier in Arlington National Cemetery, Plenty Coups was chosen to represent the Indian-Americans who had fought in World War I. He actively encouraged young Crow to acquire the white man's education, and even to be open to their religion. These do not seem to be the acts of a depressed person. Yet this is the period of which Plenty Coups said "nothing happened." It is the period in which, as he put it, "you know that part of my life as well as I do."

I cannot pretend to say with confidence what Plenty Coups really meant. His remark is enigmatic in part because it is compatible with so many different interpretations. Some of them are superficial; others delve to the heart of the human condition. Plenty Coups might have just been giving his interlocutor the brush-off, casually saying that after this there is nothing worth talking about. But what if his remark went deeper? What if it gave expression to an insight into the structure of temporality: that at a certain point things stopped happening? What would he have meant if he meant *that*? This is the question I want to address in this chapter. It is thus an inquiry into a possibility: What *might* Plenty Coups have meant? The philosopher Søren Kierkegaard has said that if there were a genuine knight of faith in our midst we would be unlikely to recognize him: in terms of outward appearance, he is just another one of our neighbors taking a stroll in the park.[6] In a similar vein, what if Plenty Coups were witness to the breakdown of happenings? What would he be witnessing? What would it be to interpret him as something more than an old chief nostalgic for a bygone past?

The question is what it would be for Plenty Coups to be a witness to a peculiar form of human vulnerability. If there is a genuine possibility of happenings' breaking down, it is one with which we all live. We are familiar with the thought that as human creatures we are by nature vulnerable: to bodily injury, disease, ageing, death—and all sorts of insults from environment. But the vulnerability we are concerned with here is of a different order. We seem to acquire it as a result of the fact that we essentially inhabit a way of life. Humans are by nature cultural animals: we necessarily inhabit a way of life that is expressed in a culture. But our way of life—whatever it is—is vulnerable in various ways. And we, as participants in that way of life, thereby inherit a vulnerability. Should that way of life break down, that is *our* problem. The suggestion I want to explore in this chapter is that if our way of life collapsed, things would cease to happen. What could this mean? And there is another aspect to our question that I want to explore: What would it be to be a witness to this breakdown? Plenty Coups seems to have become entangled in his culture's history in an extraordinary way. Obviously, he lived through a period in which the Crow abandoned their traditional nomadic-hunting way of life. But he seems to have become a spokesman from inside that way of life for the death of that way of life. What gave him such authority to speak for the way of life? Did he assume responsibility for it? And if so, how? In virtue of what did he become the designated mourner?

We live at a time of a heightened sense that civilizations are themselves vulnerable. Events around the world—terrorist attacks, violent social upheavals, and even natural catastrophes—have left us with an uncanny sense of menace. We seem to be aware of a shared vulnerability that we cannot quite name. I suspect that this feeling has provoked the widespread intolerance that we see around us today—from all points on the political spectrum. It as though, without our insistence that our outlook is correct, the outlook itself might collapse. Perhaps if we could give a name to our shared sense of vulnerability, we could find better ways to live with it.

This, then, is a work of philosophical anthropology. Unlike an anthropological study, I am not primarily concerned with what actually happened to the Crow tribe or to any other group. I am concerned rather with the field of possibilities in which all human endeavors gain meaning. This is basically an *ethical* inquiry: into how one should live in relation to a peculiar human possibility. But it also has what philosophers call an *ontological* dimension: if we are going to think about how to live with this possibility, we need to figure out what it is. What is this possibility of things' ceasing to happen? This is not, as Aristotle would call it, an inquiry that is proper to any of the special sciences: it is neither a work of anthropology nor of psychology nor of history. I do not pretend to pronounce on the deepest truths about the Crow; in particular, whether things really ceased to happen for them. The inquiry is rather into what it *would* be if it *were* true that after a certain point nothing happened. To that end, I do rely on the invaluable historical and anthropological research on the Crow as well as on oral histories: not because I want to fill out the picture of what happened to them—that is the task for some future Crow historian or anthropologist—but because I think the only satisfactory way to investigate this remarkable human possibility is to locate it in a textured historical context. The Crow actually did endure a cultural catastrophe, and looking at their actual experience may make it somewhat easier to grasp this elusive possibility of things' ceasing to happen. But the possibility that concerns me is not the special province of this or any other culture: it is a vulnerability that we all share simply in virtue of being human.

It should now be clear why a straightforward anthropological interpretation of Plenty Coups's words will also not give us what we are looking for. On the anthropological interpretation, Plenty Coups is saying that after a certain decisive event (or set of events)—the disappearance of the buffalo, being confined to a reservation—a traditional way of life came to an end. Anthropologists and historians have given us insightful accounts of what it is like for people to have to endure a breakdown in their way of life. Again, this interpretation—like the psychological interpretation before it—has the advantage of interpreting Plenty Coups as saying something plausible, and of saying something he could have plausibly believed. But on this interpretation Plenty Coups is speaking a kind of shorthand: he isn't really saying that at a certain point things stopped happening; he is giving voice to the idea that a traditional form of life ended. But what we want to know is: What is it about a form of life's coming to an end that makes it such that for the inhabitants of that life things cease to happen? Not just that it would *seem* to them that things ceased to happen, but what it would *be* for things to cease happening.

The anthropologist Marshall Sahlins has said that "an event becomes such as it is interpreted. Only as it is appropriated in and through a cultural scheme does it acquire historical *significance*."[7] Thus he can claim that "history is culturally ordered, differently so in different societies, according to meaningful schemes of things."[8] So, if we think of happenings as being given to Plenty Coups in terms of the schema of traditional Crow life, with the breakdown of that life one might well expect a similar threat to what had traditionally been counted as a happening. The anthropological interpretation of Plenty Coups's words thus seems plausible. But what does this mean? What are the conditions of its being possible?

A philosophical inquiry may rely on historical and anthropological accounts of how a traditional culture actually came to an end, but ultimately it wants to know not about actuality but about possibility: What is this possibility of things' ceasing to happen? If this is a possibility, it is a possibility we *all* must live with—even when our culture is robust, even if we never have to face its becoming actual. It is a possibility that marks us as human. How should we live with it? This question points to another difference between a philosophical inquiry and a regular empirical inquiry: ultimately, it is concerned with *ought* rather than *is*. If this is a human possibility, philosophy—in its ethical dimension—wants to know: How ought we to live with it? So: it is one thing to give an account of the circumstances in which a way of life actually collapses; it is another to give an account of *what it would be* for it to collapse. And it is yet another to ask: How ought we to live with this possibility of collapse? As we shall see, there is an important ambiguity in the words "a way of life comes to an end." And this ambiguity keeps us in the dark about what anyone might mean when he claims that "after this, nothing happened." We are trying to grasp an extreme possibility of human existence—in part so that we can grasp the scope and limits of human possibilities. Thus we want to try to understand the person making this claim—"After this, . . ."—as making as radical a claim as is humanly possible. And we want to ask, what would it be for such a claim to be true?

## Protecting a Way of Life

The Crow had no conscious understanding of this peculiar vulnerability that we are trying to track. Thus insofar as it hit them, they were not in a position to see it coming. That is, they were not in a position to understand the significance of what it was they were about to endure. We are in a somewhat better position than the Crow were—we are a literate culture that has a history of reflecting on the phenomenon of civilizations' collapsing—but still we are largely in the dark about what it would be for things to stop happening. If we reflect on how the Crow defended themselves in general, we may be able to gain insight into how they happened to protect themselves—perhaps unwittingly—against this peculiar possibility. For as long as they could sustain themselves as a vibrant tribe, they thereby held this possibility at bay. And perhaps the special circumstances of their collapse will bring this possibility to light.

The Crow were a nomadic, hunting, warrior tribe. The Crow historian Joseph Medicine Crow has hypothesized that they came into existence instantaneously. Their ancestors, the Hidatsa, had lived along the Mississippi River at the beginning of the sixteenth century, and had migrated during that century to North Dakota. One of the chiefs, No Vitals, had a vision in which he received sacred tobacco seeds from the Great Spirit, who told him to go west to high mountains to plant them. There they would flourish. For a while No Vitals and his followers settled with the Mandan along the Missouri River, but then they split off to find their promised land.

> When No Vitals left, he started out afresh as a brand-new tribe without a name; he literally and symbolically decided to travel light, for he left all heavy impedimenta behind him for good. His band became an instant tribe capable of existing as a separate and distinct entity, and one motivated with desire and dream of someday receiving the blessings of the Great Spirit when it reached the promised land![9]

The details of their migration are fascinating—and contested—but it is generally agreed that by 1700 they were settled in what is now Montana and Wyoming. To survive as a nomadic tribe, they had to be good hunters, but they also had to be good at protecting themselves against rival tribes—notably the Sioux, the Blackfeet, and the Cheyenne. Fighting battles, defending one's territory, preparing to go to war—all this permeated the Crow way of life. The Crow were and are known to themselves as Absarokee, which literally means "children of the Large-Beaked Bird." French trappers and traders took that bird to be a crow—and thus named the tribe Le Corbeau. It is generally thought that the Europeans misidentified the bird, though its exact identity remains uncertain.[10]

Robert Lowie, an anthropologist who visited the Crow at the

turn of the twentieth century and recorded the memories of those
who could remember the old way of life, described the situation
this way:

> War was not the concern of a class nor even of the male
> sex, but of the whole population, from cradle to grave.
> Girls as well as boys derived their names from a famous
> man's exploit. Women danced wearing scalps, derived
> honor from their husbands' deeds, publicly exhibited the
> men's shield or weapons; and a woman's lamentations
> over a slain son was the most effective goad to a punitive
> expedition . . .
>
> Most characteristic was the intertwining of war and re-
> ligion. The Sun Dance, being a prayer for revenge, was
> naturally saturated with military episodes; but these were
> almost as prominent in the Tobacco ritual, whose
> avowed purpose was merely the general welfare. More
> significant still, every single military undertaking was
> theoretically inspired by a revelation in dream or vision;
> and since success in life was so largely a matter of mar-
> tial glory, war exploits became the chief content of
> prayer.[11]
>
> Training for war began in childhood. Apart from athletic
> games, the boys counted coups on game animals, made
> the girls dance with the hair of a wolf or coyote in lieu of
> a scalp . . . On the subject of warfare the older genera-
> tion, otherwise little inclined to interfere with youth
> turned didactic. "Old age is a thing of evil, it is well for a
> young man to die in battle," summed up the burden of
> their pedagogy.[12]

There are two features of Crow warfare that deserve comment: the planting of a coup-stick and counting coups.[13] The paradigmatic use of a coup-stick was for a warrior to mark a boundary. Each of the clans within the tribe had its own coup-stick—and the head of the warparty of that clan would carry the coup-stick into battle. A fundamental principle of warrior honor was this: if in battle a warrior stuck his stick in the ground, he must not retreat or leave the stick. A Crow warrior must hold his ground or die losing his coup-stick to the enemy.[14] In practice, there was a complex process each year by which the officers or wise men of the clan would select the young warriors who were "made to die."[15] A member might decline this honor by saying, "I am afraid I am not strong enough"; but, conversely, a member might also be tricked into smoking a pipe before knowing that he thereby contracted to take on this role for the season. And some members of the clan would put themselves forward as "Crazy-Dogs-Wishing-to-Die": these were warriors who defiantly courted death, running right up to the enemy in a battle.[16] A Crazy-Dog was paid great respect by the tribe.

The planting of a coup-stick was symbolic of the planting of a tree that could not be felled.[17] In effect it marked a boundary across which a non-Crow enemy must not pass. This was a paradigm of courage. A warrior culture will accord highest honor to the brave warriors—and to the wise old chiefs who once were brave warriors. These were men who were evidently willing to risk their lives to protect the tribe. But there is a question of why bravery took on this particular cultural form. After all, everyone who went into battle was risking his life; and there may well have been occasions when the best military strategy would have been to retreat. Why valorize this form of standing fast? Obviously, planting a coup-stick may have been of psychological value in rallying the other warriors; it may have served to unnerve the enemy. And thus it did have military value. But there remains a symbolic element that needs to be explained. In planting the coup-stick the Crow warrior was not only risking his life; he was also in effect "saying":

> *Beyond this point, penetration by a non-Crow enemy is impossible.*

Obviously, there are possibilities that the enemy will move forward—but, if the ritual is going as it should, none of those possibilities is one in which the Crow warrior remains alive. That is, the warrior was making a show of risking *all his* future possibilities in order that this space should be protected from the enemy. Thus insofar as the warrior is in control of possibilities, he is "saying" that there is no possibility of a non-Crow's imposing his will upon the Crow. The planting of a coup-stick in this way becomes an existential declaration of impossibility. And this has the effect of "saying":

> *There is a fate worse than death.*

Namely, it is better for me to die (in a glorious battle) than for the Crow tribe to be threatened by the penetration of the boundary at this point. This "declaration" was recognized as such by all parties, friend and foe alike. The approaching Sioux enemy knew that the warrior who planted the coup-stick would protect that ground with his life. In this way, a culturally embedded form of insistence—*you may not cross this point unless you are a Crow*—became a paradigm of courage for the Crow.

Once we grasp this paradigm, it becomes easier to understand a derivative act of boundary-setting that was known as counting coups. Here is Plenty Coups's account:

> To count coup a warrior had to strike an armed and
> fighting enemy with his coup-stick, quirt, or bow before
> otherwise harming him, or take his weapons while he
> was yet alive, or strike the first enemy falling in battle, no
> matter who killed him, or strike the enemy's breastworks
> while under fire, or steal a horse tied to a lodge in an en-
> emy's camp, etc. The first named was the most honor-
> able, and to strike such a coup a warrior would often dis-
> play great bravery.[18]

The phrase "to count coup" was used ambiguously to name any of these brave acts *and* to name a ritual ceremony, after the battle, in which each of the warriors sitting in a circle *re*counted his coups: he then planted a feather in front of himself, one for each of his coups. He was then allowed to wear those feathers, either in his hair or on a coup-stick or on his shield. If a young warrior counted coup he could immediately pick a wife and marry; otherwise he had to wait until he was twenty-five years old. The wife of a coup-counting warrior could ride proudly ahead of her husband in a procession, carrying his shield; the wife of a non-coup-carrying man had to ride behind her husband. In ceremonial processions, the men who counted coups, along with their wives, rode first.

Obviously, the practice of counting coups valorized bravery—a trait that was necessary for the Crow to survive. Honor was accorded to the brave men, along with access to women, extra food, and other material benefits. Imaginative-desiring-erotic-honor-seeking life was organized around this kind of bravery.

Little boys would play at counting coups, and little girls would dance with the "scalps" that their brave boyfriends had brought them. But if we look at Plenty Coups's list, we see that more was at stake for the Crows than mere physical or even social survival. If the survival of the Crow tribe as a social unit had been the primary good, one might expect that highest honor would go to the warrior who *killed* the first enemy in battle, or the warrior who *killed* the most. But to count coup it was crucial that, at least for a moment, one *avoided* killing the enemy. There is a certain symbolic excess in counting coups. One needed not only to destroy the enemy; it was crucial that the enemy recognize that he was about to be destroyed.

In the paradigm act of counting coups, one hits one's enemy with one's coup-stick *before* harming him. This requirement suggests that the struggle is not simply for survival, but for recognition. The enemy sees that you are the victor before you strike him down. But why should this matter? Actually, what matters is that *the tribe* recognize that you got the enemy to recognize that you were the victor before you struck him down. That is what the after-the-battle ceremony of counting coups is about.

But why should this recognition-by-the-enemy matter to the tribe? It is not sufficient to say that the tribe is recognizing and rewarding the warrior's bravery. True, if the tribe accords honor in this way, then the individual young brave has a reason to strive for that honor. But why should the tribe allocate honor thus? Indeed, why should the tribe treat such an act as bravery, rather than as unnecessary, and thus as foolhardy showing off? After all, by striking the enemy first with a coup-stick, a Crow warrior puts himself at excessive risk when it comes to the task of destroying the enemy. And by putting himself at unnecessary risk, he thereby puts the tribe at unnecessary risk. For it could be that, in the moment of striking with the coup-stick, the warrior makes himself vulnerable and is killed before he has a chance to kill. The boundary line is thus breached by the enemy. Why allow—indeed, why encourage and valorize—this added risk to the tribe's survival?

It is not sufficient to say that the tribe is organized around love of honor. Even if true, why should honor be distributed *in this way?* Another culture might award honor to the warrior who kills the enemy with efficiency and skill. It might look down on counting coups as excessive risk-taking and vulgar showing off.

Aristotle says that true excellences of character—what are called the virtues—have in common that they tend to strike the mean between excess and defect. Given a particular life-challenge, a courageous person will act in a way that avoids the excess of foolhardy recklessness, on the one hand, but also the defect of cowardliness on the other.[19] The courageous person will in any given circumstances be able to find the *appropriate* way to behave courageously. This is what it is to strike the mean: to find an appropriate way to behave in circumstances in which it is possible to do too much or too little. Thus far we have focused on the excessive character of counting coups—excessive from the perspective of immediate threat to survival and well-being. But if we want to understand counting coups as a manifestation of virtue—as a paradigm of courage—we need to understand how it might nevertheless strike a mean.

Here is one way: the reality of a boundary is established when people on both sides recognize it as such. The about-to-die Sioux warrior can see that he is about to die because he has threatened a Crow boundary. He sees that this is the end of his life—his possibilities have run out—and they have run out because he has come up against a reality he cannot alter: *Crow reality*. Even he has to see this: Crow meaning has become his necessity. Seeing this is his last act. And the Crow tribe, when they celebrate their victory later that night, can see that even their most deadly enemy had to acknowledge the reality of the boundary that the Crows themselves assert. Thus an act that looks gratuitous from the point of view of physical survival is on target when it comes to the maintenance of the boundaries of Crow life.

The establishment of boundaries will, of course, be important to any cultural group. But it is especially tricky when it comes to a nomadic group whose migration depends heavily on hunting. As the tribe migrates, its defensible boundaries will shift, but it needs to be able to exert a proprietary claim over the animals within its (shifting) domain; and it needs to be able to repulse the proprietary claims of its rivals. Counting coups is the minimal act that forces recognition of these boundaries *from the other side*. The about-to-die Sioux warrior is, after all, about to die: if all goes as planned, he will be no further threat to the Crow. Recognition of the Crow boundary is the second-to-the-last thing the Crow warrior wants from him. (The last thing is his scalp, but that will serve as a token that he achieved that recognition.) If the tribe's goal is the firm establishment of a boundary, then the act of counting coups is not excessive. It strikes the mean between the defect of wishfully thinking that one has boundaries when one is unwilling or unable to defend them and the excess of slaughtering one's enemies so quickly that one does not obtain from them recognition of anything. When struck with a coup-stick, the Sioux warrior recognizes a Crow boundary because he also recognizes that he is about to die.

This is the paradigm act of counting coups, the establishment of a boundary recognized by both sides. And this paradigm is itself like a condensed version of the original act of the Crow warrior's planting a coup-stick in order to mark a boundary. Hitting him with a coup-stick is like first planting the coup-stick in order to mark a boundary; *then* one kills him because he has violated it. One can now see that all the other acts of counting coups are derivative from this paradigm. To go through Plenty Coups's list:

- Taking the enemy's weapons while he is still alive: One demonstrates to the enemy that he cannot pass this boundary *as a warrior*. Even he has to recognize that he lacks the means.

- Strike the first enemy in battle, no matter who kills him: This is the equivalent of planting a coup-stick. One thereby declares that beyond this point he shall not pass, no matter who kills him. (It makes sense that this should not be the highest form of counting coups.) Similarly for

- Striking the enemy's breastworks while under fire.

- Stealing a horse from the enemy's camp: Obviously, there was some material benefit in stealing a good horse. But, as the anthropologist Robert Lowie noted, a successful Crow warrior had more horses than he could use. The horses often served as a sign of success.[20] But success at what? In the case of stealing a horse, it again served to mark a boundary. In seeing that his horse had been stolen—from under his nose—the enemy had to recognize that he was at the edge of Crow country; for his horse—or what had been his horse—was now a *Crow* horse.

"Plenty Coups" is a translation into the contemporaneous frontier argot of the Crow name Alaxchiiaahush, which means "Many Achievements." His grandfather gave him that name after having a dream-vision in which his grandson would have a long life and count many coups. He was originally named Bull Goes into the Wind (Chiilaphuchissaalesh) by his mother.[21] The story of his first coup was legendary. His beloved older brother had been killed in an expedition against the Sioux. Alaxchiiaahush, then a young boy, was devastated—and sought revenge. He waited a few years, until he was sixteen; then he and his partners sneaked up on a Sioux hunting party. As a Sioux warrior was chasing a wounded buffalo, young Plenty Coups waited until the warrior was almost upon him, sprang to his feet, jumped the Sioux, and scalped him alive. The author who recorded this incident comments: "Far more merciful to have sent an arrow down into his heart. Never could that scalped Sioux hope to become a warrior. He was disgraced; he would be ostracized by his tribe, forced to wear the dress of a squaw, and must henceforth crawl through life in utter ignominy. The mark of the coward was upon him."[22]

Young Plenty Coups inflicted on this wretched Sioux a fate worse than death. But the revenge goes beyond the humiliation of this warrior. For as the Crow tribe celebrated this coup, they would recognize that even the Sioux who mocked this man had to recognize—indeed, did recognize in the very act of mocking—that the Crow had made their mark. For as long as he lived, he would be a living witness to the reality of the Crows.

The anthropologist Robert Lowie noted with puzzlement that while it was "meritorious" to kill an enemy, it was even better to tap him with a coup-stick. "Obviously the idea was not primarily to reduce a hostile force but to execute a 'stunt,' to play a game

according to whimsical rules . . . The coup was indeed interpreted in so conventional a way that often it bore no relation to
true bravery whatsoever."[23] The point of mentioning this comment is not to ridicule what in 20-20 hindsight looks like the paro-
chial outlook of an anthropologist working a century ago. It is to
highlight the fact that we cannot understand what bravery is unless we grasp the goals that the bravery is in the service of. If the
Crows wanted to secure a boundary and grasped that doing so requires recognition of the boundary from both sides, then counting coups—as Aristotle would say, in the right place, at the right
time, and from the right motivations—does count as brave.

### Gambling with Necessity

The Crow recognized that in planting the coup-stick and counting coups they were trying to protect a space in which Crow life
could flourish. At the very least, they were aiming to protect the
tribe against devastation. The threats were real and imminent.
The historian Richard White, building on the research of other
historians and anthropologists, has argued convincingly that it is a
mistake to think that the master historical narrative of this period
is of a stable, traditional society being overwhelmed by the advance of western civilization. Such a narrative overlooks the significance of intertribal warfare: "wars were not interminable con-
tests with traditional enemies, but real struggles in which defeat
was often catastrophic":

> The history of the northern and central American Great
> Plains in the eighteenth and nineteenth centuries is far

more complicated than the tragic retreat of the Indians
in the face of an inexorable white advance. From the
perspective of most northern and central plains tribes the
crucial invasion of the plains during this period was not
necessarily that of the whites at all. These tribes had few
illusions about American whites and the danger they
presented, but the Sioux remained their most feared enemy.[24]

This is not the place to tell the history of the terrible military pressure that the westward migration of the Sioux placed on the
Crow, but, as White describes, the hunting grounds around the
Yellowstone, Rosebud, and Big Horn Rivers, which had been
dominated by the Crow in the first half of the nineteenth century,
were "reduced to a neutral ground in the 1840s and 1850s."[25] And
it was certainly part of living memory for the rest of the century
that, in the early 1820s, a thousand Sioux warriors had launched a
surprise attack on a Crow village near the Yellowstone River and
destroyed several hundred lodges. According to oral tradition,
half of the population was killed.[26] In principle, every bearer of a
coup-stick was willing to give his life so that something like that
should never happen again.

The Crow had been fighting the Sioux for decades, but, as
White points out,

By the 1840s . . . the once formidable Crows were a
much weakened people. As late as the 1830s they had
possessed more horses than any other tribe on the upper
Missouri and estimates of their armed strength had
ranged from 1,000 to 2,500 mounted men, but the years
that followed brought them little but disaster. Smallpox

and cholera reduced their numbers from 800 to 460
lodges, and rival groups pressed into their remaining
hunting grounds.[27]

The historian Frederick Hoxie titled his chapter on this period
"Life in a Tightening Circle." In brief, it is a story of painful
choices made against a background of external threat and ever-in-
creasing confinement. At the beginning of the century, the Crow
were surrounded by enemy tribes—the Sioux, Cheyenne, Arap-
aho, and Blackfeet—and all of them increasingly realized how
dependent they were on knives, hatchets, tools, and guns for survival. The Crow hunted beaver in the first half of the century,
buffalo in the second—in large part to be able to trade their fur
and hides for American- and European-made goods. By the 1850s
the Crow were regularly facing attacks by the Sioux from the east
and the Blackfeet from the north. As Hoxie puts it, "The era of
vague borders and friendly mountain men was over . . . To be
without guns, blankets and ammunition in the Yellowstone in the
1850s was suicide."[28]

This is the period in which Plenty Coups grew up: it is the period in which, by his own account, things were still happening.
Even this thumbnail sketch of the historical context should suf-
fice to show that the Crow not only knew what they were fighting
for; they also had a vivid sense of what they were fighting against.
They were fighting to prevent *utter devastation* at the hands of the
Sioux. This was the prospect of a Crow holocaust: a weakened
tribe being fatally overrun by the Sioux. In this worst possible scenario, men, women, and children would be slaughtered—the
tribe would be exterminated—with perhaps a few survivors taken
into captivity as slaves. This was a very real possibility. It is in this

context that the Crow tribe decided to ally with the white man, in particular the U.S. government, in what became a common battle against the Sioux.

It seems clear, then, that the Crow were living within a world of possibilities that they understood fairly well: they understood what it was for them to flourish; what it was for them to survive and cope with the challenges of hunting, disease, and war; what it was to face the prospect of utter devastation. It is worth dwelling for a moment on this extreme possibility of destruction. Had there been a Crow holocaust it would have been fair to say that a way of life had come to an end—at least, in some familiar sense of those terms. The tribe would have been destroyed; there would no longer be any people to carry out their traditional rituals. Still, if we think of the inner life of the one surviving Crow slave, he would have the conceptual resources to understand what had happened to himself and his people. This worst possible scenario was one that he well understood. And, however unrealistic, his dreams of escape, revenge—of planting his coup-stick again!—would make complete sense to him, as well as to his Sioux masters. Let us assume that there was no chance of this dream's coming to fruition: still, the possibility it describes would continue to make sense.

This is enough to show that the type of devastation the Crow actually endured as they willingly moved onto the reservation in the 1880s was of a different order from anything for which they could thoughtfully plan. When one talks about "the world of the Crow," one might mean various things—though in general one is referring to a context of rituals, traditions, ways of living. But one hallmark that one is dealing with *a world* is that relevant in-

stances of the law of excluded middle apply to it. So, of an upcoming battle everyone in the tribe implicitly knew:

> *Either our warriors will be able to plant their coup-sticks*
> *or they will fail.*

This is a typically Crow instance of the law of excluded middle,
and it was related to a family of others, for example: "Either we
shall celebrate our victory tonight or we shall be mourning our
dead." Obviously, the Crow did not self-consciously formulate
laws of logic. But their lives were organized in ways that manifested certain basic commitments. This distinctively Crow instance of the law of excluded middle is future oriented, and
it purports to cover *all* future possibilities. Looking ahead, the
Crow do not know whether they shall succeed or fail in planting
the coup-stick—thus they have the idea of a world that is not fully
under their control—but they do know that they shall either succeed or fail. For in battle any lack of success is a failure. From the
Crow perspective, nothing is being left out: these are all the possibilities there are.

It is just this assumption—that they have covered the field of
possibilities—that breaks down for the Crow when they move
onto a reservation. This is what they cannot see coming, because they assume they already have in view all the possibilities
there are. That is, they take themselves to have in view the arena
in which success or failure occurs. The anthropologist Marshall
Sahlins has said that every culture is a "gamble played with nature"—in the sense that it depends on the continued availability
of environmental resources, and on challenges that it can continue to negotiate.[29] The Crow gambled on the continued avail-

ability of buffalo and other animals to hunt; they knew that their existence depended on their ability to fight off the Sioux. But there was a different kind of gamble that they didn't understand: a *gamble with necessity.* This is a gamble that the entire field of possibilities will remain stable; that one will continue to be able to judge success or failure in its terms. This is what came under pressure. As we shall see, the very intelligibility of the Crow version of the law of excluded middle came into question.

### Was There a Last Coup?

Against a background of unrelenting pressure from the Sioux, the Crow signed the first Fort Laramie Treaty in 1851, in which the United States recognized their right to 33 million acres of what is now Montana and Wyoming. It also promised to pay the tribe $50,000 worth of supplies per year. But, as Frederick Hoxie points out, there were neither enforcement procedures nor established penalties for failing to comply. The United States paid out this amount once. The 1860s were a period of terrible wars with the Sioux. In 1867 the United States negotiated a second Fort Laramie Treaty, in which it recognized only 25 percent of the land recognized in the first treaty: Crow lands were reduced to 8 million acres. During this period, the Crow fought on the side of the United States against their common enemy, the Sioux; and they inflicted significant damage. But the emerging peace on the northwest plains only increased the immigration of white settlers, and thus placed increased pressure on Crow lands. In 1882 Crow land was reduced again, to about 2 million acres. And in the period 1882–1884 the Crow—their resources depleted, threatened by disease, cold, and starvation—moved to a reservation. Intertribal warfare was forbidden by the U.S. government. Hunting became impossible, both because all the beaver and buffalo had been killed and because the Crow were now forbidden to pursue a nomadic life. There was also devastating mortality. As Hoxie points out, nearly one-third of the 2,461 Crows recorded in the 1887 census died in the 1890s, as a result of a confluence of poor sanitation in new conditions of confinement, lack of ability to resist diseases carried by white settlers, and malnutrition. The younger generation was all but wiped out. Not surprisingly, those who survived suffered massive disorientation. Ambitious young men, wishing to establish themselves in the tribe, could think only in terms of warfare—but warfare had been forbidden. There were sporadic intertribal attacks, but overall the young men had a sense that they had come too late to participate in the Sioux wars.[30]

Things came to a head in the fall of 1887. Nearly every detail of what happened has been subject to contesting interpretations, but in broad strokes an incipient rebellion was crushed. In the summer of 1887, members of the Blackfeet tribe had stolen horses from the Crow, thus inflicting a tribal insult. A group of young Crow, led by Wraps His Tail, set out to get revenge and count coup. On September 30 they returned exultant: they had captured Blackfeet horses and were parading them through the camp. On some earlier occasion this would have been a classic act of counting coups. There was, apparently, much shouting and shooting of guns into the air. At one point, Wraps His Tail, who was then twenty-five, rode up to the agency interpreter, Tom Stewart, and stuck a gun into his belly. He then pulled it away, and fired into the air. In another time, and *if* the whites had been their enemy, this would have counted as a further coup. It is not clear whether the much-hated agent, H. E. Williamson, came out to confront the crowd or whether Wraps His Tail rode up to him; but, in any case, shots were fired in his presence, going over his head, over the rooftops of the houses, but hitting the bricks of a chimney.[31] The young men then rode away.

What began as a traditional celebration to count coup went badly wrong. Williamson reacted to this outburst by declaring that the original act of taking horses from the Blackfeet was "horse-stealing," and he ordered the young men arrested. *Blankets and Moccasins* is written in the genre of a wild-West tale, and one of the authors had befriended Chief Pretty Eagle, one of the participants in the event. So the account may be distorted; still, it has the advantage of giving us the outlook of someone who lived through those events:

> The bewildered young leader who had anticipated a
> warm welcome with feasting and dancing found himself ·
> in unaccountable disgrace. Passionately those Indians re-
> sented the seeming injustice of the arrest. According to
> their ethics of warfare they had conducted themselves
> admirably. They were no horse thieves; they were war-
> riors. Having invaded the enemy's camp and fought a
> successful battle they had returned with booty.[32]

Pretty Eagle made a trip to the rebels' camp to try to talk some sense into them. Wraps His Tail was angry about the overall threat to the traditional Crow way of life, but he was also upset about meaning: "They call us 'thieves' . . . They, the palefaces, who make treaties only to break them, who have stolen our buffalo and our land, they call us 'thieves.'"[33]

Throughout the opening weeks of October, memos went back and forth between the Crow Agency and the Indian Office in Washington. And, in the region, fears were rising among the white population that Wraps His Tail was trying to form alliances with their traditional enemies, the Sioux, Blackfeet, and Cheyenne, to provoke a massive Indian uprising. Whatever efforts Wraps His Tail made in this direction, it does not seem he had much success. Nevertheless, by October 20 the U.S. secretary of war dispatched a general and troops to put down this potential uprising. By November 4, the U.S. cavalry was ready to meet this band of young rebels with overwhelming force. There was a short skirmish, and almost all the young men surrendered. Wraps His Tail tried to escape, but he was found by a member of his own tribe—Fire Bear, who worked as a policeman for the Crow Agency. The circumstances of his death are contested; but it seems clear that Fire Bear shot him in the head at point-blank range. On one credible account, Wraps His Tail's father had found him and was bringing him back to the agency as a captive when Fire Bear shot him.[34] Fire Bear was ostracized from the tribe for the rest of his life. At Crow Agency he is reviled to this day.

This is a classic case of what the historian Richard White has called the closing of a middle ground.

> The middle ground is the place in between: in between cultures, peoples, and in between empires and the nonstate world of villages . . . On the middle ground diverse peoples adjust their differences through what

amounts to a process of creative, and often expedient,
misunderstandings . . . They often misinterpret and dis-
tort both the values and the practices of those they deal
with, but from these misunderstandings arise new meanings and through them new practices—the shared meanings and practices of the middle ground.[35]

It seems clear that the Crow participated in creating such a middle ground from the beginning of their encounters with white
traders. François Antoine Larocque, a French-Canadian trader,
who first encountered the Crow in 1805, brought them axes and
knives, but also smoked tobacco with them and told them that
the "Chief of the White people" wanted to make them "his Children and Brethren." His description of tribal life had, as Hoxie
puts it, "all the precision of a shareholder's prospectus"; while, for
their part, the Crow engaged in the ritual of adopting him. "It was
clear to Larocque that the protocol of trade required the familial
greetings he saw going on around him."[36] It is this kind of toler-
ance of a space of competing meanings that itself came under attack at the end of the nineteenth century.

As Wraps His Tail provoked unrest, he was renamed Sword
Bearer by some of his followers, and he came to have that name
among whites. There are different accounts of how Sword Bearer
acquired his sword, and thus his name; but he used it to promote
a myth of invincibility.

> "This sword," he said, brandishing the bright steel blade
> over his head, "was sent me by the Great Spirit. Once
> while I was on the mountain top making strong medi-
> cine it came floating down to me from the Blue. While I

carry it nothing can harm me or any of my followers—
no poisoned arrow—no white man's bullets."[37]

Apparently, he had been able to predict a thunderstorm with uncanny success; and when lightning struck, he lifted his sword and
claimed that he had brought it down. He claimed to be responsi-
ble for the malfunction of U.S. guns; and in so doing, he became
a symbol of hope for those who wanted to hold on to traditional
Crow meanings. After all, if the Crow had been chosen by God to
have this land, it made sense that something like this should be
happening. The point is not to make any ethical claims about
how Wraps His Tail should or should not have been treated.[38] It is
only to say that in crushing him, the government simultaneously
crushed the space in which traditional Crow meanings might survive unchallenged.

It is tempting to say that the struggle was over who could tell
the narrative: Was he a brave warrior who counted coup, had
great medicine, and fought for the Crow? Or was he a young
troublemaker who stole some horses and tried to cause mayhem?
Obviously, there is a significant issue of how historical narratives
are shaped by the victor. But that is not the only significant issue
here. And we should not let this issue of narrative blind us to a peculiar form of devastation that the Crow had to endure. For the
issue that concerns us is not who has the power to tell the story—
however important that might be; it is rather how power shapes
what any true story could possibly be. Once the U.S. government forbids intertribal warfare—and demonstrates that it has the
power to enforce this prohibition—the possibility of counting
coups evaporates. Counting coups makes sense only in the context of a world of intertribal warfare; and once that world breaks

down, *nothing* can count as counting coups. This isn't just a matter of who tells the story. If a young Crow were today to sneak over to the Sioux reservation and take a horse, this would be a cause for sadness *among the Crow*. They would recognize that there is no longer anything to celebrate or recount.

We do not grasp the devastation that the Crow endured so long as we think that the issue is who gets to tell the story. For the problem goes deeper than competing narratives. The issue is that the Crow have lost the concepts with which they would construct a narrative.[39] This is a *real loss*, not just one that is described from a certain point of view. It is the *real loss of a point of view*. This is the confusion of the young man who takes the horse: he has not yet recognized this loss. For an act is not constituted merely by the physical movements of the actor: it gains its identity via its location in a conceptual world. And it is the world which has broken down. The very physical movements that, at an earlier time, would have constituted a brave act of counting coups are now a somewhat pathetic expression of nostalgia.[40]

Similarly, nothing can any longer count as planting a coup-stick. One can take what used to be a coup-stick and stick it in the ground—but *nothing* follows from that. And it is utterly unclear what one would be doing. There is no boundary that is being protected; no life is being risked. The Crows' nomadic life is over, and insofar as there is a Crow boundary it is recognized and protected by the U.S. government and the State of Montana. The planting of a coup-stick has ceased to be an intelligible act—in the sense that there are no longer viable ways to do it. The only ways of living forward with it are retrospective: one can remember it, recount its history, dramatize it at a powwow, mourn its loss. But—as things now stand—there is no way to plant it. Without living possibilities, it can no longer function as a coup-stick.

There is reason to think that Plenty Coups recognized this change. Frederick Hoxie describes a special moment at the ceremonial burial of the Unknown Soldier in the fall of 1921. Plenty Coups had been invited to Washington to represent the Indian nations.

> After the chaplain had completed his prayers, Plenty Coups stepped forward. Dressed in brilliantly beaded buckskin, carrying a coup stick, and wearing an eagle-feather headdress, the seventy-two-year-old warrior's presence was a stunning match for the European generals and the officers from the Mikado's navy who stood in the front ranks of the audience in their polished boots and gold braid. The huge crowd watched in absolute silence as the . . . leader—who had first come to Washington with Pretty Eagle and Medicine Crow more than forty years before—removed his war bonnet and laid it on the sarcophagus along side his coup stick.[41]

What was he doing with his warbonnet and coup-stick? Many meanings might attach to such a gesture; but in the context of the current discussion one meaning suggests itself: *he is burying them.* On this interpretation, Plenty Coups is serving as a remarkable kind of witness: he is marking the end of a way of life in which the coup-stick and warbonnet had integral roles. They have reached the end of their traditional lives, and it is time to locate them in a new ritual, that of remembering and mourning the valiant deeds of Indians past.

### Witness to Death

Planting a coup-stick and counting coups were culturally embedded forms of insistence. In their Crow-like way, they insisted upon the reality of Crow life. Even the enemy had to accept this reality. When the enemy failed, they were confronted by the courage, the obduracy, of the Crow; when the enemy succeeded, they still had to reckon with the coup-stick as an obstacle to be overcome. And Crow life had reality because it could be insisted upon. As we have seen, this form of insistence set out a field in which success or failure had to lie. It is one thing for this form of insistence to fail, in the sense of being overrun by the enemy. This is a failure that is anticipated within the form of insistence itself. It is quite another for the form of insistence to fail, in the sense of ceasing to be an intelligible act. What we have in this case is not an unfortunate occurrence, not even a devastating occurrence like a holocaust; it is a breakdown of the field in which occurrences occur.[42] If we go back to our paradigm instance of the Crow law of excluded middle,

*Either our warriors will be able to plant their coup-sticks or they will fail,*

we can see that it was meant to parcel out all possible future occurrences.

There are basically two ways of responding to this breakdown of intelligibility. One is to preserve the validity of this instance of the law of excluded middle by reinterpreting failure in ways that extend beyond anything the Crow could have imagined. That is, ". . . or they will fail" is now interpreted to mean:

> *Either they will fail in the traditional ways or they will*
> *fail in the sense that the very act of planting a coup-stick*
> *will become unintelligible.*

On this reading, any non-planting of a coup-stick becomes a failure to plant one. And thus, if the act becomes unintelligible or absurd, that, too, counts as a failure. This is not the route Plenty Coups took—at least, as I am interpreting him. The Crow form of insistence has become unintelligible: even he can no longer insist in a Crow-like way. As I have interpreted him, he is the great Crow leader who, ironically, acknowledges that it is no longer possible to insist in the way that a great Crow leader would. But even if these peculiarly Crow forms of insistence are no longer possible, Plenty Coups may continue to insist that these are the terms in which the world makes sense. Thus if

> *Either our warriors will be able to plant their coup-sticks*
> *or they will fail*

*as traditionally understood* does parcel out all future happenings, then, with the breakdown of the intelligibility of this instance of the law of excluded middle, there is a breakdown in what might count as a happening.

Thus burying the coup-stick is not just a dramatic gesture. And we can now see how this crisis of happenings could spread out from the battlefield and permeate the rest of Crow life. During the period of vibrant nomadic life, everything was somehow related to hunting and war. All the rituals and customs, all the distribution of honor, all the day-to-day preparations, all the upbringing of the children were organized toward these ends. The flourishing life for the Crow was one of unfettered hunting of beaver and buffalo. It occurred in a land that they understood to be given them by God; and the presence of a rare tobacco was a divine sign that this was indeed their land. Battle was a means of protecting this way of life; but it was such an essential part of life that much of life's meaningful activities were related to it.

To take one example we have already encountered:

> The Sun Dance, being a prayer for revenge, was naturally saturated with military episodes.

What is one to do with the Sun Dance when it is no longer possible to fight? Roughly speaking, a culture faced with this kind of devastation has three choices:

1. Keep dancing even though the point of the dance has been lost. The ritual continues, though no one can any longer say what the dance is *for*.

2. Invent a new aim for the dance. The dance continues, but now its purpose is, for example, to facilitate good negotiations with whites, usher good weather for farming, or restore health to a sick relative.

3. Give up the dance. This is an implicit recognition that there is no longer any point in dancing the Sun Dance.

At the end of their nomadic life, the Crow gravitated toward this third option. The Crow seem to have given up their Sun Dance around 1875—about a decade before they moved onto the reservation. In 1941, after a sixty-six-year hiatus, the Crow wanted to reintroduce the Sun Dance, but the steps of the Crow version no longer existed in living memory. So the tribal leaders sought out the leaders of the Sun Dance among the Shoshone tribe in Wyoming. Thus the Crow learned the steps that their traditional enemies had danced when they had hoped to defeat the Crow in battle.[43]

Plenty Coups lived through the period when the Crow stopped dancing the Sun Dance; and he died before it was re-introduced. It is thus possible to interpret his claim "After this, nothing happened" as an assertion that after moving onto the reservation no traditionally important events like the Sun Dance happened any more. But it is also possible to hear him as bearing witness to a deeper and darker claim: namely, that no one dances the Sun Dance any more because it is no longer possible to do so. Once planting a coup-stick loses meaning, so, too, does the Sun Dance. One might still teach people the relevant steps; people might learn how to go through the motions; and they can even call it the "Sun Dance"; but the Sun Dance itself has gone out of existence.

The Sun Dance was a prayer-filled ritual asking God's help in winning military victory. This is not something that can intelligibly be performed now. At best, one could perform "it" as a nostalgic gesture: an acted-out remembrance of things past.[44] If there could be a Sun Dance there would be a happening. Or if normal preparations for a Sun Dance were halted in traditional ways— say, the family seeking revenge was given adequate compensation from the enemy tribe—that, too, would be a happening. But what doesn't count as a happening is the breakdown of the concepts in terms of which people understand things to be happening. Concepts get their lives through the lives we are able to live with them. If nothing any longer can count as dancing a Sun Dance or planting a coup-stick, then the tribe has lost the concepts Sun Dance and coup-stick. This is how I interpret Plenty Coups's witness: to a loss that is not itself a happening but is the breakdown of that in terms of which happenings occur.

Everything in tribal life was organized around hunting and war—but hunting and war have become impossible. There is a crucial ambiguity in this claim that is easily overlooked. When we say "It is no longer possible to go to war" or "It is no longer possible to hunt buffalo" we might mean either:

> *Circumstances are such that there is no practical possibility of our performing those acts*

or

> *The very acts themselves have ceased to make sense.*

By way of analogy, consider a person who goes into her favorite restaurant and says to the waiter, "I'll have my regular, a buffalo burger medium rare." The waiter says, "I'm sorry madam, it is no longer possible to order buffalo; last week you ate the last one. There are no more buffalo. I'm afraid a buffalo burger is out of the question." Now consider a situation in which the social institution of restaurants goes out of existence. For a while there was this historical institution of restaurants—people went to special places and paid to have meals made and served to them—but for a variety of reasons people stopped organizing themselves in this way. Now there is a new meaning to "it is no longer possible to order buffalo": no act could any longer count as ordering. In general these two senses of impossibility are not clearly distinguished because they often go together. In the particular case we are considering, it is in considerable part because the buffalo herds were destroyed—and thus hunting them became impossible in one sense—that the Crow agreed to move onto a reservation and abandon their traditional way of life—and thus hunting them became impossible in this other sense.

Plenty Coups said that after the buffalo went away nothing happened; and we can now begin to see what he might have meant.[45] If planting a coup-stick (or failing to plant it), counting coups (or failing to count coups), and performing a ritual like the Sun Dance (or failing to) were the only things that counted as events, then it would make sense to say that after the buffalo went away things ceased to happen. From the perspective of traditional Crow life—and this is the life in which the concept *counting coups* acquired its meaning—nothing can any longer count as either performing or failing to perform the deed.

So far we have considered the tribe's valorous acts and major rituals. But what about simple acts like cooking a meal? People continued to prepare meals on the reservation. Why doesn't that count as something happening? Is there a way that Plenty Coups's haunting claim might take even such a simple act into its compass? Imagine an evening in 1860: a young Crow woman wanders by another's teepee, sees her stirring a pot on an open flame, and asks her, "What are you doing?" She answers, "I'm getting my husband and family ready for tomorrow's battle."[46] In the context, this answer is a real possibility. She is preparing a meal, but she identifies the act by locating it in a larger scheme of purposefulness. It is this larger scheme that is suddenly wiped out—and with it goes the possibility of identifying the act in this way. In 1890, it is still possible for a member of the Crow tribe to stir a pot outside a teepee, and such stirring can count as cooking a meal. But there are no longer any circumstances in which an appropriate answer to the question "What are you doing?" is "Getting my family ready for tomorrow's battle." Now suppose one were a witness to the demise of traditional Crow life. One might well feel the need to stand witness to the demise of this possibility. How might one do so?

One way would be to insist that every event in Crow life—even cooking a meal—gained its significance within the larger framework of Crow meaning. Such a witness would insist that in traditional Crow life there was no such thing as the bare cooking of a meal. Every meal was in effect the cooking-of-a-meal-so-that-those-who-ate-it-would-be-healthy-to-hunt-and-fight. At a certain point, though, hunting and fighting have become impossible. Indeed, they cease to be intelligible acts. (A young man could still sneak off the reservation with a bow and arrow; he might even kill an elk; but these actions no longer count as hunting as traditionally understood.) But if hunting and fighting become unintelligible, so does *preparing* to hunt and fight. Nothing can any longer count as doing that. But in traditional Crow life, *everything* counted either as hunting or fighting or as preparing to hunt and fight. Thus, even as simple an act as cooking becomes problematic. Obviously, the Crow continued to cook meals. And, if asked, they could say what they were doing. And, if asked further about it, they could say that they were trying to survive, trying to hold their family together from one day to the next, and so on. But a witness to the demise of a way of life might want to insist that these are not genuine happenings.

Let us use the term "temporality" as a name for time as it is experienced within a way of life. Humans may mark time by the regular movements of the sun and moon, by the approach of day and night, by the passing of the seasons; they may make sundials and clocks; they may invent symbolic systems, calendars, by which the passage of time can be marked; and so on. Heidegger has argued that temporality is always *datable* in the sense that a given time is always a time *when* . . .[47] It is a time when there were heavy snows, a time when we were preparing to fight against the Sioux, a time when Plenty Coups counted his first coup. Aristotle says that time is a measure of change and rest. We mark that change with a *now*—a now that divides the change into a before and an after.[48] But to grasp this now we need to understand it as a now-*when*: a now when *this change* is occurring. But in the situation as we are envisaging it, the Crow ran out of *whens*: the categories that would normally have filled in the blanks lost their intelligibility. It could no longer be a now-when-we-are-hunting-buffalo. And nothing could any longer count as now-when-we-are-preparing-for-such-a-hunt. Similarly for battle. But all Crow temporality had fitted within these categories—everything that happened could be understood in these terms—and thus it seems fair to say that the Crow ran out of time.

Obviously, the members of the Crow tribe still inhabited some minimal form of temporality. They could of course grasp that nomadic life was in their past; and they were aware of such moments as now-when-we-are-struggling-to-get-our-rations. But this was not a category in their way of life. It was a description that arose as a symptom that that way of life was devastated. Above all, it didn't amount to anything: there was no larger framework of significance into which it could fit. One can now see how a witness to the demise of that way of life might nevertheless declare his allegiance to it by insisting that the breakdown of Crow temporality does not itself count as a happening.

## Subject to Death

If the traditional Crow experienced devastation in things they might do, they also experienced a terrible attack on what they might be. If we consider a vibrant culture, it is possible to distinguish:

1. *Established social roles.* These will include socially sanctioned forms of marriage, sexual reproduction, family, and clan; standard social positions such as warrior, squaw, medicine man, and chief; ceremonial rituals; and so on.

2. *Standards of excellence associated with these roles.* These give us a sense of a culture's own ideals: what it would be, say, to be really outstanding *as a chief, as a squaw, as a warrior, as a medicine man.*

3. *The possibility of constituting oneself as a certain sort of person—namely, one who embodies those ideals.* I shall call such a person a *Crow subject.* This is what young Plenty Coups aspired to: to be a chief, to be outstanding as chief, and thus to be a living embodiment of what it was to be a Crow.

Of course, the word "subject" has a variety of related meanings. But I want to put it to a special use. The idea of being a Crow subject that I want to explore is more demanding than contemporary ideas of cultural identity or identification. We tend to think of identity in terms of social roles or religious, racial, or gendered categories.[49] So, in contemporary American society there are categories such as *black, African-American, Hispanic, Jew, gay*—and of course *Native American*. These identities are socially available categories, and one may be assigned to one irrespective of one's conscious choice. Identification implies some kind of acceptance of one's socially assigned identity. One takes the identity to provide a (partial) answer to who one is. In brief, not that much is required to inhabit such an identity or identify with such a group. In this sense, the Crow tribe has of course survived as a social group, and the members of the tribe may identify with being a Crow.

The idea of a Crow subject requires more than this sort of identification. It requires internalizing the ideals associated with the standards of excellence associated with social roles. And it requires making those ideals a life's task. To take an example from traditional Crow culture, being a Crow warrior *subjectively understood* was not just a matter of occupying the social role of Crow warrior. Nor was it merely a matter of being extremely good at being a Crow warrior—understood as a social role. That is, it was not enough merely to be very good at killing Sioux in battle, and so on. To be a Crow subject one had to fulfill these conditions, but one also needed to constitute oneself as a person for whom living up to the relevant ideals constituted who one was. This was more than a mere psychological matter of "identifying" oneself in a particular way. It required a steadfast commitment stretching over much of one's life to organize one's life in relation to those ideals. And it required a certain success in doing so. That is, being a Crow subject required more than inhabiting a social role, being excellent in that role, and even identifying oneself in those terms. It required all these things, but in addition it required a lifelong commitment to shaping oneself to be this kind of person. Subjectivity, so understood, is a never-ending task.[50]

If we think of Plenty Coups, for example, he knew from childhood that he wanted to be a chief, and he trained himself in the skills, habits, and excellences associated with being a great warrior and then a great chief. It is not just that he achieved the social role of chief, nor that he was very good at it, nor that he identified with his role. Being a Crow chief went to the heart of who he was. He took the ideals associated with being a chief and made them his own. Living up to those ideals was his life's task. It was not a project he could accomplish once and for all. In childhood he was aspiring to be someone who could instantiate those ideals—and rather than settling for wishful daydreams, he applied himself to acquiring the skills that would make his dreams come true. In early manhood he became a great warrior—and everything in his life was organized around being one. Later in life he at least tried to live up to the ideals of a chief in times of rapid change and cultural devastation.

The problem is what happens to the subject when the possibility of living according to its associated ideals collapses. The social group may endure, and one may be able to identify with being a member of that group—thus a member of the tribe can still think of him- or herself as a Crow—but the possibility of constituting oneself as a certain sort of subject suddenly becomes problematic. One symptom of this is that at such a historical moment *a peculiar form of irony will first become possible.* By 1890 the tribe was ensconced on the reservation and intertribal warfare was forbidden. One could now ask:

*Among the warriors, is there a warrior?*

This is not a question that would have made sense among the Crow circa 1850. Of course, one might have been able to say something mildly ironic like "You haven't met a warrior until you've met Plenty Coups." But this trope requires a clear sense of what is involved in being a warrior. It would not have made sense to ask whether anyone in the group of warriors was a warrior. One wouldn't have known what was being asked, precisely because the ideals associated with being a warrior were clear and it was beyond doubt that the best warriors instantiated them.

Similarly, once the tribe moved onto the reservation it became possible to ask:

*Among the chiefs, is there a chief?*

Although there were traditional chiefs when the Crow moved onto the reservation, over time it became unclear what a chief was supposed to do. Obviously, chiefs were supposed to lead; but until this moment leadership had been understood in terms of proven ability to lead in battle and hunts. One could of course look back with reverence to the great leaders of the past; but nostalgia or retrospection only defers the question: What counts as real leadership now? Since the old criteria for choosing a chief are no longer viable, it is essentially unclear on what basis new chiefs should be chosen. And it is also unclear how one might adjudicate this question. The Crow struggled with this problem. When Plenty Coups died in 1932, "the head men of the Crow council voted unanimously against choosing another chief. The leader of the council said . . . 'No living man can fill Plenty Coups's place.'"[51] It is part of contemporary oral tradition among some Crow that this story has been romanticized. According to this account, the Indian agent Calvin Asbury wanted to ensure that no particularly powerful individual figure took Plenty Coups's place, and he asked his allies on the Crow tribal council to put forward such a motion. Even if this account is true, the fact that he was able to succeed shows that the Crow were confused about what, if anything, could count as criteria for being a chief in these new circumstances.

Revealingly, there isn't quite the same pressure on the question:

*Among the squaws, is there a squaw?*

For the traditional role of a squaw centered upon supporting the family and raising children—and these roles would be required more than ever in the challenges of reservation life. Even so, squaws paradigmatically supported men in their warrior roles: the wives of brave warriors painted their faces and paraded in front of their husbands, holding their coup-sticks and shields. They raised their children in ways that would prepare them for a life of hunting and war. All of this was no longer possible. And it is clear that the problem was not simply a breakdown of traditional roles: basic patterns of upbringing were threatened. "I wonder how my grandchildren will turn out," Pretty Shield confided to Linderman in 1931. "They have only me, an old woman to guide them, and plenty of others to lead them into bad ways. The young do not listen to the old ones now, as they used to when I was young. I worry about this, sometimes."[52]

All in all, by 1940 one could raise a question that would have been incomprehensible in 1840:

*Among the Crow, is there a Crow?*

This is a form of irony that is at the same time earnest.[53] In asking it, I do not mean to add insult to injury. I want rather to look at a condition that any of us might face. The reason this form of irony was impossible for the Crow in 1840 is that the various criteria for being a Crow hung together unproblematically. Indeed, the unquestioned cohesion of these criteria was a sign of the vibrancy of traditional Crow life. But with the onset of reservation life, all three of these criteria came under pressure—and so did their ability to cohere. Some social roles (1) remained relatively constant—like that of squaw—but it became increasingly problematic what a warrior was, what it was to perform a traditional ceremony, and so on. The problem became acute because the standards of excellence associated with those roles (2) all but evaporated. There was no longer a clear sense of what it would be to be outstanding as a chief. And thus there was no longer any obvious way to constitute oneself as a Crow subject (3). If the culture's traditional ideals became unlivable, the possibility of constituting oneself as a Crow subject must have become problematic. If it is no longer possible to live this way of life, there is no longer a way to be a person who is excellent at living that life. It is under these conditions that this form of irony starts to make sense. For in the first part of the question,

Among the Crow . . . ,

the word "Crow" picks out the social group as determined by (1); while in the second part of the question,

. . . is there a Crow?

the word refers to the Crow subject, the person who constitutes himself according to the standards of excellence, (2) and (3). It is because these criteria have come apart that a special form of irony becomes possible. This, I think, shows the peculiar challenge that faces anyone whose civilization is under pressure. For if one is straining to live, and to help others, in a worthwhile way, the question can no longer be, say, "How shall I, as a Crow, go on?" but "What shall it be for me to go on *as a Crow?*" And one is forced to address this question at a time when it is no longer clear how one could possibly answer it.

This is a problem that penetrates deeply into one's inner life. As a *very* rough analogy—and a flight of fancy—imagine that pieces of a chess game had inner lives. And imagine that each took itself to be a center of agency.[54] *I am a knight!* I see myself in tribal terms: *I am a black knight! I am proud to be a black knight! We shall fight a glorious battle and capture the white king!* I think strategically in terms of my possible moves: two up and one to the right, two up and one to the left. *Perhaps I should wait here quietly for several moves, and if that white rook comes my way . . .*[55] I understand all the other members of my tribe in terms of the roles they play: and I understand that we are all aspiring to excellence in the sense that we are *trying to win.* Unbeknownst to me, my world exists because it is protected by a group of humans. These are the guardians of the chess world, who insist that the only acceptable moves are moves that are allowable within the game of chess. From my point of view as a thoughtful knight, the humans are as unknowable as the transcendent gods. But suppose these chess-guardians were one day just to give it up: as a historical phenomenon, humans got bored with playing this game, and the game of chess goes out of existence. My problem is not simply that my way of life has come to an end. I no longer have the concepts with which to understand myself or the world. I understood the other pieces in terms of their roles, but there are no longer any such roles. Perhaps I am found attractive by humans as a physical object. I am put on a bookshelf as a curiosity, an objet d'art. I might sit for generations on a series of bookshelves—

get traded as what humans call an antique—and all this while I am in utter confusion. I have *no idea* what is going on. This isn't primarily a psychological problem. The concepts with which I would otherwise have understood myself—indeed, the concepts with which I would otherwise have shaped my identity—have gone out of existence.

Obviously, the situation is much more complex—and charged—when it comes to human societies and cultures. Typically, a culture will be in some kind of contact with neighboring cultures; and the Crow were interacting with whites at least from the beginning of the nineteenth century. Still, the admittedly crude analogy is of use because it brings to light the intimate connection between thinking and being. Part of what it is to be a Crow subject is to be *aiming* at being excellent as Crow; it involves *intending* to plant one's coup-stick; *hoping* that the buffalo herd will be good this year; *desiring* to acquit oneself well in the hunt; *wondering* whether one will participate in the Sun Dance; and so on. But if Crow subjectivity collapses, so does the possibility of having any of these mental states. As it turns out, intending and hoping and wondering and desiring are not just up to me: they are not just a matter of exercising my will. And my inability to do so is not just a psychological issue: it is a question of the field in which psychological states are possible. To make the point, allow me to speak in the first person as an imaginary Crow subject: Not only can I no longer plant a coup-stick, but nothing could count as my intending to do so. As it turns out, only in the context of vibrant tribal life can I have any of the mental states that are salient and important to me. The situation is even worse: these are the mental states that help to constitute me as a Crow subject. Insofar as I am a Crow subject there is nothing left for me to do; and there is nothing left for me to deliberate about, intend, or plan for. Insofar as I am a Crow subject, *I* have ceased to be. All that's left is a ghostlike existence that stands witness to the death of the subject. Such a witness might well say something enigmatic like "After this, nothing happened."

## The Possibility of Crow Poetry

The interpretation I have worked out is bleak. I do not pretend to say that this is what happened to the Crow. Nor do I know that this is what Plenty Coups meant by his utterance. Perhaps he meant something else; perhaps even if he meant this he was mistaken in his judgment. All I have done is to work out in a radical but plausible way what it would be for him to have been saying something true. What I am concerned with is an *ontological vulnerability* that affects us all insofar as we are human. I have focused on the Crow in part because Plenty Coups's words happened to haunt me; in part because it is at least arguable that they actually did have to suffer in these ways. This helps us to imagine vividly—and I think accurately—what it would be like for this human possibility to be realized.

One of the ironies that comes to light is that groups of people can be the bitterest of enemies in real life, yet ontologically they are on the same side; and a real-life ally can turn out to be one's ontological nemesis. The Crow and the Sioux were bitterest of enemies; and if either side could have they would gladly have destroyed the other. Still, their standoff sustained a world in which battles, planting coup-sticks, and counting coups all made sense.

One has only to read Chief Sitting Bull's pictorial autobiography to see that he was every bit as much concerned with counting coups as Plenty Coups was.[56] And yet, with the United States as an ally—a questionable and unfaithful one to be sure, but still an ally in many ways—the Crow moved into a position in which their world fell apart.[57]

In working out this interpretation, I have not wanted to foreclose on human hopefulness. In particular, I do not want to foreclose on hopefulness *for the Crow*. Indeed, much of the rest of the book will examine Plenty Coups's hopefulness—what it was and what might justify it. But, for the moment, let me simply say that in claiming that planting a coup-stick lost intelligibility—that nothing could count because the possibilities of doing such had been exhausted—I do not mean to imply that nothing could ever count as doing such again. What would be required, though, would be a new Crow poet: one who could take up the Crow past and—rather than use it for nostalgia or ersatz mimesis—project it into vibrant new ways for the Crow to live and to be. Here by "poet" I mean the broadest sense of a creative maker of meaningful space. The possibility for such a poet is precisely the possibility for the creation of a new field of possibilities. No one is in a position to rule out that possibility.

With this possibility in mind, one can see Plenty Coups's gesture in yet another light. He is witnessing the death of the Crow subject, to be sure—but he does so in order to clear the ground for a rebirth. For if the death is not acknowledged there will most likely be all sorts of empty ways of going on "as a Crow." Only if one acknowledges that there is no longer a genuine way of going on *like that* might there arise new genuine ways of going on *like that*. This impasse would explain Plenty Coups's eagerness to tell his story to a white man. For in a time of cultural collapse, living memory of that living way of life will last only a few years. The most important artifact the white man could offer the Indian—much better than guns—was writing and printing. In the *Phaedrus*, Socrates argues that writing can function as a form of forgetting rather than remembering: for it can lull one into thinking that one is remembering when one is only moving the phrases about. Whatever the dangers here, when one's whole way of life is on the verge of collapse, the worry about writing becomes a luxury. The entire culture is in the process of being forgotten; the only hope is to write it down in the hope that future generation may bring "it" back to life.

Plenty Coups was a witness to the collapse of the Crows' future: he witnessed a time in which "nothing happened." Such a witness manifests a new and intensified form of Crow subjectivity: he takes on the responsibility of declaring whether the ideals around which he has shaped his life are any longer livable. That is, he is willing to speak for the health and viability of the old ways of constituting oneself as a subject.[58] But this can be done in the hope of clearing the ground for the creation of new forms of Crow subjectivity. There is reason to think that Plenty Coups told his story to preserve it; and he did so in the hope of a future in which things—Crow things—might start to happen again.

# II

## ETHICS AT THE HORIZON

### The End of Practical Reason

THE CROW HAD A conception of happiness, a conception of what life was worth living *for*. They lived in relation to a spiritual world in which they believed God had chosen them to live a certain kind of life. Happiness consisted in living that life to the full. This was an active and unfettered pursuit of a nomadic hunting life in which their family life and social rituals could prosper. Because the tribe was threatened by other tribes, they developed a warrior culture to defend their way of life. The martial values—bravery in battle, the development of the appropriate character in young men, and the support of the warriors by all the tribe—were important constituents of happiness as understood by the Crow. With the destruction of this way of life came the destruction of the end or goal—the *telos*—of that life. Their problem, then, was not simply that they could not pursue happiness in the traditional ways. Rather, their conception of *what happiness is* could no longer be lived. The characteristic activities that used to constitute the good life ceased to be intelligible acts. A crucial blow to their happiness was a loss of the concepts with which their happiness had been understood.

A number of tribal leaders gave voice to this confusion. The medicine woman Pretty Shield told Linderman, "I am trying to live a life that I do not understand."[1] And Two Leggings, a lesser chief, gave a similar account of life on the reservation: "Nothing happened after that. We just lived. There were no more war parties, no capturing of horses from the Piegan and the Sioux, no buffalo to hunt. There is nothing more to tell."[2] We have already encountered Plenty Coups's extraordinary claim: after the buffalo "went away," he said, "you know that part of my life as well as I do." In general, we think it constitutive of a person having *a life* that he or she claims some authority over saying what is happening in it. Plenty Coups had his wits about him; his sensory faculties were intact: he could certainly say what he was doing. His problem was that the central concepts in terms of which his life would have gained significance in his eyes—counting coups, planting a coup-stick, hunting buffalo, fighting off the Sioux— became unlivable. That is why he could tell a white man "you know that part of my life as well as I do": the categories in terms of which Plenty Coups would have lived his life had become uninhabitable. The categories that remained were equally available to white man and Indian; they were not the ones with which Plenty Coups would have chosen to tell *his* story. And yet, these were the circumstances in which he was called upon to act.

### Reasoning at the Abyss

It was in these conditions that Plenty Coups had to think about how to live—indeed, about how to lead his tribe. But, in such circumstances, practical reason is deprived of important resources. Candace Vogler has argued that when we try to think ahead practically we are either thinking about how to achieve some end; or thinking about what is a fitting way to behave; or thinking about how to sustain some pleasure.[3] That is, practical reason always aims toward what is useful, toward what is proper or appropriate behavior, or toward what is pleasant. In the transition to reservation life, there was still room to deploy all these forms of practical reason. The Crow no doubt thought about how to obtain food and shelter in these new circumstances, about whether it was proper to send their children to the white man's schools, and about how to sustain whatever pleasures might be available on the reservation. Nevertheless, there was relatively little for practical reason to get hold of.

In the absence of a livable conception of the good life, the scope of practical reason became attenuated. As we saw in the previous chapter, when the Crow were a vibrant nomadic tribe, even an everyday occurrence like cooking a meal potentially opened out onto a way of life. At least in principle such an act could be redescribed as "getting ready for a hunt," "getting ready for a battle," "getting ready to move on," or "making sure we're ready for tonight's dance." But with the destruction of the *telos*, there was no conception of the good life to provide a larger context for the significance of one's acts. People continued to prepare meals, but now it was only cooking-in-order-to-survive. This, I suspect, was what Two Leggings meant when he said, "Nothing happened after that. We just lived." People continued to act practically, but they lost the rich framework in which such acts made sense.[4]

To take a historical example: in the context of nomadic life it made sense to keep one's horses in good shape. But with the collapse of that life, it became problematic why horses should continue to matter. Obviously, they might have continued to matter in nostalgic terms, but in that case their role would have become sentimental. The historian Joseph Medicine Crow describes a terrible blow the tribe endured when, in the 1920s, the U.S. government, in response to complaints from white farmers, decided to destroy all the so-called wild horses on the western plains. These included horses roaming on the Crow reservation that the tribe considered their own. This slaughter was done against the wishes of the tribe, and it caused much pain.

> In the first slaughter the government said that about forty thousand head were exterminated, but the Crows said it was many more, including many tame ranch horses, which the gunmen preyed on when it got difficult to find wild ones. Thus by 1930 the great and proud horse people, the Absarokee, were bereft of horses. When the horse was gone the Crow culture was severely damaged. To say the least, this was a traumatic and tragic experience for a proud horse-oriented tribe; it was worse than actual military defeat, which some Plains tribes sustained.[5]

If we are willing to face this pain and ask what it was about, it is not sufficient to say that this was the pain of impotent rage; the rage of seeing that one could not stop the slaughter of the tribe's beloved horses. Nor is it sufficient to say that it was pain at the destruction of the traditional way of Crow life. All this may be true, but there was a special cruelty that remains to be named. This was the pain of being forced to recognize that one's traditional way of life was *already* over. One may complain about the destruction of the horses, but one can no longer give the reason that would hitherto have given legitimacy to the complaint: that the horses were *needed* for the maintenance of the Crow nomadic-hunting-warrior life. Part of the pain was being forced to recognize that no one could any longer say what horses were for.[6]

A similar puzzlement arises around the idea that it was *fitting* for the Crow to have fine horses. This sense of what was a proper source of pride had been embedded in a vibrant conception of the good life. When that good life became unlivable, it became unclear on what basis anyone could say whether or not it was fitting to have fine horses. The question of how it befitted one to act continued to arise—alas, it arose in ways that pressed hard upon them—but they had been deprived of the framework in which they could have given a traditional answer. When the Crow were a vibrant nomadic tribe, the paradigmatic virtue was courage. It always and everywhere befitted a young Crow man to behave courageously. But the paradigmatic understanding of courage was in terms of a warrior culture. Courage was bravery in battle—above all, planting a coup-stick and counting coups. That is, the virtue of courage was understood in terms of the *thick* concepts of Crow culture.[7] Other forms of behavior counted as courageous—for example, bravery on a hunt that suddenly became dangerous—but all of these were oriented around the Crow paradigms of bravery in battle. Thus practical reason was able to engage with the question of what befitted a Crow warrior: what kinds of acts were disgraceful, what would bring honor, what kind of dress was appropriate for such a person, how he should comport himself in camp, and so on. The problem was what to do when the way of life collapsed. It could no longer be fitting to

plant a coup-stick if the very act of planting a coup-stick had become an impossible act. But then how was one to think about appropriate behavior?

It was in the context of cultural collapse that Plenty Coups hit
upon an extraordinarily fitting act. At the Tomb of the Unknown
Soldier he ceremonially laid down his coup-stick. As I suggested
in the previous chapter, he was burying it. Given the life the tribe
had lived with the coup-stick, this was what it was appropriate to
do with it now. But this extraordinary act makes the general point.
There was still room in these radically altered circumstances to
think about what it was appropriate to do. And it was still possible
to formulate a stunning answer. Nevertheless, what made Plenty
Coups's act so uncannily appropriate was that he symbolically expressed the thought that the traditional modes of fitting behavior
themselves had to be laid to rest. It had become appropriate to express the demise of traditional understandings of what was appropriate.

One would expect that with a traditional society like the Crow
there would be more stability among the social roles accorded
women. Even with the collapse of the nomadic way of life, there
were still meals to cook; there were still families that needed support. Yet in the written records of women's experiences there is
also expression of confusion. Agnes Yellowtail Deernose said of
this period, "Destruction of the buffalo and the shift to a reservation left young men and women in a state of social limbo."[8] And
Pretty Shield related a poignant event. In traditional upbringing, she said, "We talked to our children, told them things they
needed to know, but we never struck a child, never." Then she
paused.

"Lately I did strike a child," she said grimly. "There seemed to be nothing else to do. Times and children have changed so. One of my grand-daughters ran off to a dance with a bad young man after I told her she must not go. I went after her. It was a long way too, but I got her, and in time. I brought her home to my place and used a saddle-strap on her. I struck hard, Sign-talker. I hope it helped her, and yet I felt ashamed of striking my grandchild."

It is at that point that she said, "I am trying to live a life I do not understand."[9] Notice the mixture of shame and confusion. Shame is one of the basic emotions by which we regulate our sense of what is and what is not appropriate behavior. It originates in very early experiences of feeling exposed.[10] Over time it is disciplined by the culture's sense of what is appropriate and disgraceful. Pretty Shield felt ashamed because she had been brought up in a culture in which one *never* struck a child—and yet there she was thrashing her granddaughter. This moment would never have occurred if the old culture had remained stable. She was not someone who would have had cause to feel shame, for she was not someone who would ever have struck her granddaughter—but for the breakdown of a way of life. So she felt the shame that would have accompanied a beating in the old world; but she also recognized that she saved her granddaughter from one of the emerging degradations of reservation life. Yet she did so in the context of a life she did not understand—and thus did not know how to evaluate.

I do not know which of her granddaughters Pretty Shield

thrashed. But one of her granddaughters—I suspect a different one—wrote a memoir of her grandmother. Alma Hogan Snell reports that her grandmother *regularly* complained, "I'm living a life I don't understand":

> She would lament, "I'm living a life I don't understand."
> She would be working and talking—then immediately
> she would fall silent. She would continue to work, but
> she was silent. I would be with her, and I would sit silent
> and wait for her. I became accustomed to that, so I was a
> very quiet individual at times. Then she'd come up with
> this sound she always made, "Hummmm, aaahh." She
> said it mournfully, like this thing that she was thinking
> about in her mind was so overwhelming; "Why has this
> thing come upon us? Now we are made to say 'yes' and
> 'no.' When the white man comes to us, we just naturally
> say 'yes.' We are not obligated to take what he has, but
> my children, my grandchildren are always right there to
> say, 'Yes, we'll do it. We'll do it.' They seem to like to do
> it. They seem to like what they see. I feel like I am losing
> my children to this new world of life that I don't know."[11]

It is difficult to imagine a more articulate expression of mourning for the demise of a culture's sense of what is fitting.[12]

## A Problem for Moral Psychology

There is also a question of how one could be psychologically equipped to face a cultural collapse. As far back as Plato and

Aristotle, thinkers in the western tradition have emphasized the importance of early childhood training for character-formation. And, as we saw in the first chapter, the Crow agreed.[13] Children were brought up in ways meant to instill the excellences of character as understood by the Crow.[14] These traditions may have differed on particular virtues—or excellences—but they agreed that the virtuous person is one who has the capacities of character and body that enable him or her to lead an excellent and happy life. These traditions also agreed that it is through training and habituation that a person's character is shaped—in particular, the character and outlook of a virtuous person. This outlook is deeply ingrained, and it is psychologically stable. Such a person will have not only a view of what is excellent, noble, and fine—but also a view of what is shameful. This view is not *just* a view: it is a psychologically ingrained nexus of perception and motivation. A virtuous person does not require the actual humiliation of others to experience shame. He or she will naturally avoid shameful acts. Virtuous people not only seek fine acts; they are highly motivated to avoid shameful acts. And they are good at anticipating what might bring on shame. A courageous person, for example, not only will have good judgment about what counts as a shameful act; he will rule out such acts as impossible (for him). If one has been brought up, say, in the patterns of Crow excellence, one will likely have an internalized shame-mechanism that reflects the Crow understanding of courage.

But what if actual historical circumstances make that understanding of courage no longer a possible way to live? If we consider this moment of historical crisis, it seems as though there ought to be courageous ways to face the breakdown of traditional forms of courage. But if we take a person's psychological makeup into account, there is a serious question of how a courageous Crow could make that courageous transition. Everything in his training has facilitated the formation of a solid psychological structure. He can't just change it as a matter of will or decision. A person's character is not directly under his conscious control. Part of what it is to be courageous is to see the world in certain sorts of ways. If he has been trained since childhood to see certain acts as shameful, how can he in a moment come to see that shame is really no longer the appropriate response? This is the problem: If he has been trained from earliest youth that courage consists in going on *like this* . . . , it is not clear how we can expect him to make the psychological changes needed to see things differently.

This is a problem for moral psychology. If, roughly speaking, we believe *ought* implies *can*: if we think that in these challenging times people ought to find new ways—not just of surviving—but of living *well*, we need to give an account of how it might be psychologically possible to do so. It would be depressing news indeed to learn that, should a civilization collapse, there might nevertheless be decent ways to go forward—but the best people of the civilization would be the least equipped to find them. Is it in the lineaments of our psychological natures that my flourishing as a member of my culture makes me *less* able to confront the challenges of a radically new future?

When the Crow were confined to the reservation they were confronted with a stark choice: either they had to give up the idea that there was any longer a courageous way to live, or they had to alter their conception of what courage was. How might one viably take this latter option? The question is not just about the psychological feasibility of anyone's making this transition; there is also a question of its legitimacy. Courage is a state of character that is manifested in a committed form of living. And commitment necessarily has a temporal dimension. In the normal course of events, a courageous person would have to maintain fidelity to his past: the courageous Crow warrior would draw upon the traditions in which he was brought up as he determined how and when to take his next step. Clearly, with the sudden transition to reservation life, there was no longer any obvious way to do that. But confronted with the thick concepts of an alien culture, how could any of them be recognized *as courageous?* If one were simply to leap from the thick concepts of one's culture into the ethical concepts of another culture, it would seem that one would experience not only a radical discontinuity with one's past; one would experience a rip in the fabric of one's self. If we think of the self as partially constituted by its most basic commitments, then in jettisoning those commitments one would be disrupting one's most basic sense of being.[15] It is hard to imagine any courageous way of doing *that*.

The question thus becomes as urgent practically as it is significant theoretically: Might there be a certain plasticity deeply embedded in a culture's thick conception of courage? That is, are there ways in which a person brought up in a culture's traditional understanding of courage might draw upon his own inner resources to broaden his understanding of what courage might be? In such a case, one would begin with a culture's thick understanding of courage; but one would somehow find ways to *thin it out*: find ways to face circumstances courageously that the older thick conception never envisaged. The issue would then be one not simply of going over to the thick concepts of another culture, but of drawing on their traditions in novel ways in the face of novel challenges. If this is a possible act, it would be good to know what kind of psychological adjustments make it possible. I want to argue that Plenty Coups did make just this sort of transformation.


## The Interpretation of Dreams

The Crow had an established practice for pushing at the limits of their understanding: they encouraged the younger members of the tribe (typically boys) to go off into nature and dream. For the Crow, the visions one had in a dream could provide access to the order of the world beyond anything available to ordinary conscious understanding. Young Plenty Coups took the traditional resource of seeking a dream-vision, and with some help from the elders in the tribe he put it to a new use. This gave the tribe resources for thought—for practical reasoning—that would not have been available to them in any other way. And it gave Plenty Coups the resources for a transformation of the virtue of courage.

In seeking a dream-vision, a young man would typically take a sweat-bath and go off to a remote spot and fast. This venture was supposed to induce receptiveness to a significant dream. Young Plenty Coups was called to go off and dream when he was nine years old. The year was 1855 or perhaps 1856. He went to a mountaintop. On the first night he had no dream, so he chopped off a piece of his finger to encourage a vision.[16] Such behavior was not unusual. Lowie reports that at the beginning of the twentieth century it was difficult to find an adult male Crow with all his digits.[17] Apparently, a typical prayer to God began with a plea, "Pity me!"

And it was thought to help if one could present oneself as deserving pity. Plenty Coups told Linderman that he knew he was following a tradition in which other Crow warriors in previous generations had "sacrificed their flesh and blood to dream."[18]

The Crow, like other American Indian tribes, had a theory of dreams. They took dreams to be meaningful: revealing—often in enigmatic form—an order in the universe that was typically hidden from ordinary conscious life. They recognized that dreams were related to their wishes. Indeed, they sought dreams as a means of getting some sort of authoritative word on whether or not their wishes would be gratified. According to Two Leggings, the Crow distinguished four different levels of dreams:[19]

> "No-account dreams," in which one merely saw some incident.

> "Wish-dreams," which saw some hoped-for circumstance coming true. These did have special spiritual power— "medicine"—but they did not always come true.

> "Property dreams," in which a person would see horses, blankets, or the like, which he would later acquire through actual events.

> "Medicine dreams" or visions. These gave powerful insight into the future.

One would expect a young chief to seek a vision in order to determine whether this was a good time to go off to battle. One would also expect young men to seek visions to know where one could hunt the buffalo herds. So the Crow, like Freud, thought that dreams were responses to human wishes. They also, like Freud, thought that the deeper meaning of dreams was often not trans-parent—and thus that important dreams required the interpreta-tion of wiser, older members of the tribe. Within the context of our inquiry, the most important difference between Freud and the Crow is that Freud thought humans were alone in the uni-verse, and the Crow did not and do not. For Freud dreams are simply a human response to human wishes: they provide a dis-guised gratification.[20] For the Crow, by contrast, humans have a meaningful place in a meaningful world.[21] Not only is the world populated by spirits, but there is a single God, Ah-badt-dadt-deah. Given this worldview, when a Crow had a strong desire or a wish, there was reason for him to hope that his desire or wish had come into being because the world itself was slightly out of kilter. Going off into the mountains to pray to God to "Pity me!" was a way of drawing the spiritual world's attention to one's plight. In a dream-vision one might be visited by a spirit who would explain just how the order of the world would be adjusted so as to gratify one's wish. Thus the Crow used dreams to find out whether they would obtain real-life gratifications.

What is striking about young Plenty Coups's dream—and the interpretation the tribe gave to it—is that it was used not merely to predict a future event; it was used by the tribe to struggle with the intelligibility of events that lay at the horizon of their ability to understand. Dreams were regularly used by the Crow to predict the future. People would, for instance, wait for a vision in a dream to tell them it was a propitious time to go into battle.[22] But young Plenty Coups's dream was of a different order. It did not predict any particular event, but the change of the world order. It was prophetic in the sense that the tribe used it to face up to a radically different future.

On his second night in the wilderness, young Plenty Coups had this dream: He sees a Buffalo-bull who he knows is a Person who wants him. He travels to a certain place, and the Bull turns into a Man-person wearing a buffalo robe. He follows him by sinking into a hole. He sees countless buffalo. He is led among them, then back out into the sun. Man-person shakes his ceremonial red rattle.

"Look!" he pointed.

Out of the hole in the ground came the buffalo, bulls and cows and calves without number. They spread wide and blackened the plains. Everywhere I looked great herds of buffalo were going in every direction, and still others without number were pouring out of the hole in the ground to travel on the wide plains. When at last they ceased coming out of the hole in the ground, all were gone, *all!* There was not one in sight anywhere, even out on the plains. I saw a few antelope on a hillside, but no buffalo—not a bull, not a cow, not one calf, was anywhere on the plains.

I turned to look at the Man-person beside me. He shook his red rattle again. "Look!" he pointed.

Out of the hole in the ground came these bulls and cows and calves past counting. These, like the others, scattered and spread on the plains. But they stopped in small bands and began to eat the grass. Many lay down, not as a buffalo does but differently, and many were spotted. Hardly any two were alike in color or size. And the bulls bellowed differently too, not deep and far-sounding like the bulls of the buffalo but sharper and yet weaker in my ears. Their tails were different, longer, and nearly brushed to the ground. They were not buffalo. They were strange animals from another world . . .

"Do you understand this which I have shown you, Plenty-coups?" he asked me.

"No!" I answered. How could he expect me to understand such a thing when I was not yet ten years old?

During all the time the Spotted-buffalo were going back into the hole in the ground the Man-person had not once looked at me. He stood facing the south as though the Spotted-buffalo belonged there.[23]

There is another part of the dream that deserves mention at this point. The Man-person invites Plenty Coups to look at a very old man sitting in the shade of a particular tree. "I felt pity for him because he was so old and feeble. 'Do you know him, Plenty-coups?' he asked me. 'No,' I said . . . 'This old man is yourself, Plenty-coups . . .' There is then a tremendous storm in which the Four Winds begin a war against the forest. All the trees are knocked down, but one."

"Listen Plenty-Coups," said a voice. "In that tree is the lodge of the Chickadee. He is least in strength but strongest of mind among his kind. He is willing to work for wisdom. The Chickadee-person is a good listener. Nothing escapes his ears, which he has sharpened by constant use. Whenever others are talking together of their successes and failures, there you will find the Chickadee-person listening to their words. But in all his listening he tends to his own business. He never intrudes, never speaks in strange company, and yet never misses a chance to learn from others. He gains successes and

avoids failure by learning how others succeeded or
failed, and without great trouble to himself . . . The
lodges of countless Bird-people were in the forest when
the Four Winds charged it. Only one person is left unharmed, the lodge of the Chickadee-person. Develop
your body, but do not neglect your mind, Plenty-coups.
It is the mind that leads a man to power, not strength of
body."[24]

Obviously, allowances need to be made for the fact that this is the
dream of a youth being recounted by an old man. It is likely
that there have been revisions in the telling and retelling of the
dream. On the other hand, this dream was recounted to the tribe
at the time. The tribe may itself have collectively revised the
dream in various ways. Nevertheless, the fact that he recounted
his dream in public when he was nine, and that the tribe immediately incorporated the dream into its own self-understanding,
gives us confidence that, in the broad scale at least, this was a
piece of imaginative activity going on at the time.

In the dream, the dreamer recognizes that he is not able to
grasp its meaning. It is as though the dream itself is calling attention to its own significance. The young dreamer, exhausted from
his ordeal, was brought back to the tribe amidst much rejoicing.
In a formal setting, the boy recounted his dream to the wise men
of the tribe. It is fascinating to see how the Crow used dreams co-
operatively. The young men were sent out to dream; and at a later
ceremonial occasion the old men interpreted the young men's
dreams. The tribe relied on what it took to be the young men's
capacity to receive the world's imaginative messages; it relied on
the old men to say what these messages meant.

The elders of the tribe listened to young Plenty Coups's dream.

Yellow Bear, "the wisest man in the lodge," offered this interpretation:

> "He has been told that in his lifetime the buffalo will go
> away forever," said Yellow-bear, "and that in their place
> on the plains will come the bulls and cows and calves of
> the white man. I have myself seen these Spotted-buffalo
> drawing loads of the white man's goods. And once at a
> big fort . . . I saw cows and calves of the same tribe as the
> bulls that drew the loads.
>
> "The dream of Plenty-coups means that the white
> man will take and hold this country and that their
> Spotted-buffalo will cover the plains. He was told to
> think for himself, to listen, to learn to avoid disaster by
> the experiences of others. He was advised to develop his
> body but not to forget his mind. The meaning of this
> dream is plain to me. I see its warning. The tribes who
> have fought the white man have all been beaten, wiped
> out. By listening as the Chickadee listens we may escape
> this and keep our lands."[25]

Although the Crow had been interacting with fur traders
throughout the nineteenth century, and the tribe was certainly
aware of the challenges that the white man posed for the Indian,
it is also clear from this interpretation that by the mid-nineteenth
century the Crow tribe still had little exposure to the white man's
way of life.[26] Yellow Bear was considered wise in part because, by
Crow standards, he had traveled far and wide. He had actually
seen the "spotted buffalo" pulling the white man's wagons. More
important, he had been to the white man's fort and there seen
cows and calves "of the same tribe" as the bulls. He had seen that

the white man had a way of reproducing the spotted buffalo. This, said Yellow Bear, was the wave of the future.

So it seems that for the Crow, dream-interpretation consisted in showing how the vision embodied in a dream applied—or would come to apply—to reality. At the time of the dream the buffalo on the plains were still plentiful, but the Crow had reason for concern. As Richard White has pointed out, the average number of buffalo robes shipped down the Mississippi River increased from approximately 2,600 robes in 1830 to about 50,000 in 1833. In 1848 a local priest estimated that 110,000 robes were shipped downriver.[27] The buffalo were disappearing from traditional Sioux hunting grounds, and as a result the Sioux were pressured to move in on the Crow. It is in this context that young Plenty Coups had his dream—and it was in this context, too, that the tribe took the dream as a key to the challenges they had to face. They decided on a foreign policy that would guide their acts for the next century. They explicitly recognized in an official council that their buffalo-hunting way of life was coming to an end, and they decided to ally with the white man against their traditional enemies. This is the way they hoped to weather the oncoming storm and hold onto their land.

### Crow Anxiety

The Crow used dreams to extend the reach of practical reason— but it was not a straightforward extension. The Crow did not treat dreams simply as a box of extra information that was locked away during ordinary waking life. The Crow took dreams as providing access to a spirit-filled realm; and it is a hallmark of this world that it is not fully intelligible in human terms. It is thus constitutive of receiving a message from the world of spirits that the message remains somewhat enigmatic.[28]

Consider the Crow account of their origin as a tribe. It is a tale of message, enigma, and resolution. According to tradition, God came to the first Crow leader No Vitals in a vision, transformed himself into a tobacco plant, and decreed that the Crow should plant this in the spring and dance with it.[29] "The people I am making shall live all over the Earth, but those to whom I give this plant shall be few and it shall make them strong."[30] The tobacco in question is a rare variety, *Nicotiana multivalvis*, that was not actually smoked by the Crow. It was treated as sacred. It is part of Crow oral history that after No Vitals received his vision, the Crow split off from the Hidatsa tribe and began migrating from what is now Minnesota, first up to Canada (the site of Alberta), then as far south as Utah, then east to Okalahoma, then northwest up through Nebraska and South Dakota into Wyoming and Montana. Joseph Medicine Crow thinks that the migration took about a century. Of course, it is not certain at what point the story of No Vitals' vision entered Crow life. Perhaps it really did occur at the beginning of the Crow tribe, just as described; perhaps it occurred at some time during their migrations; perhaps it occurred after they settled in what is now Montana. The point is that whenever it arose, it had to be linked to the Crow migrations. The Crow knew that they were a people chosen by God; and they knew that their special relation to God was bound up with their ability to plant and harvest this rare tobacco. But where was the land on which this tobacco could be grown? That was left unclear. It was only after an extended migration that they came to what they took to be the Promised Land. The Crow could make sense of their own experience only if they treated the original vision as enigmatic. Only retrospectively—when their migration had ended—could they understand what had been given to them in the beginning. Thus, from the beginning of their existence as a tribe, the Crow had a tradition of living with enigmatic oracles.

In this context, young Plenty Coups's dream provided a poignant counterpart to this original vision. Just as No Vitals' vision predicted the beginning of Crow history as a nomadic tribe, so Plenty Coups's dream predicted its end. That is, it predicted the demise of a way of life. This was a further reason for treating the dream—*and its interpretation*—as enigmatic. If their way of life was coming to an end, if a huge storm was coming, the dream itself gave them reason to think that there was much about what was going to happen that they did not yet understand. They took themselves to be receiving divine guidance; and they grasped that if they followed this guidance they would survive. Still, they had reason to think they didn't really know what this meant. For the dream told them that the entire forest would be destroyed. Though their tree—the tree of the Chickadee—would remain standing, they had reason to be puzzled about what a deforested world would be like. Plenty Coups was told in the dream that, to survive, he must follow the example of the Chickadee. The Chickadee is a bird that learns from others. But exactly what he needed to learn was left unclear. Thus although the Crow treated Plenty Coups's dream as giving them the means for survival, there was much about the dream that had, for them, to remain enigmatic. Because of their general understanding of dreams, the Crow would have received Plenty Coups's dream *as oracular*. Because they took the dream to be a message from the spiritual realm, because the message came in dreamlike form, and be-cause the dream predicted a change in their entire way of life, there was reason for members of the tribe to think that they could have only a limited understanding of what the dream was *about*. Thus it is fair to say that Plenty Coups's dream was a manifesta-tion of anxiety.

In the western philosophical tradition, anxiety is treated as an emotion or affect that has no specific object.[31] Sometimes it is said that anxiety is "about nothing," but this claim seems too strong. Rather, with anxiety there is a systematic and enigmatic unclarity as to what it is about. Anxiety would thus have been an appropriate response of people who were sensitive to the idea that they were living at the horizons of their world. For if a people genuinely are at the historical limit of their way of life, there is precious little they can do to "peek over to the other side." Pre-cisely because they are about to endure a historical rupture, the detailed texture of life on the other side has to be beyond their ken. In the face of such a cultural challenge, dreaming provides an unusual resource. It enables the dreamers to imagine a radi-cally new future without becoming too detailed about what this future will be.

In the abstract, one can imagine a member of the tribe getting up from the campfire and saying, "That's it, then: buffalo are out; farming is in. Where can I buy some seeds?" But realistically, such an abrupt act was out of the question. In part, this was be-cause the tribe paid attention not only to the content of the dream but also to the form of its delivery. It was given to Plenty Coups—and thus to the Crow—*as a dream*. By interpreting the dream as anxious, we acknowledge that the Crow lacked a firm grasp of what it was about. Clearly, the Crow used Plenty Coups's dream to plan for the future. Indeed, they saw the dream as taking them into the future. And they saw the dream as foretelling an entirely new way of life for them. But their recognition that they were interpreting a dream also gave them a way of acknowledging their meager understanding of what it was they were envisaging.

It is possible, then, to see Plenty Coups's dream as a response to a communal sense of anxiety, as well as an indication of how they moved forward in the face of anxiety. Plenty Coups told the story of his childhood as one of growing up enthusiastically in the midst of vibrant Crow life. This was a sincere account of his conscious memory of an innocent childhood. But, as we have already seen, the period was also one in which the tribe had to cope with devastating disease as well as terrible enemy onslaughts. The Sioux had been more resilient to smallpox than the Crow; and thus a fierce population confronted them in greater numbers. Both the Sioux and the Blackfeet were actively trading for weapons; and so the Crow, on the one hand, were constantly being pressured to give up ground; while, on the other hand, they were pressured to increase their trading, and thus their dependence upon traders and their goods.[32] It is not unreasonable to suppose that a sensitive nine-year-old was attuned to the anxiety in his community and that he was able to dream what he was not yet in a position to think. And he dreamt it on the tribe's behalf.

Plenty Coups's dream seems to have been an integral part of a process by which the tribe metabolized its shared anxiety. It helps, I think, to conceptualize the anxiety not as specifically located in this or that person but as diffused throughout the tribe. It is the tribe that is anxious. Or, perhaps even more accurately, a way of life is anxious—though it cannot yet say what it is anxious about. Young Plenty Coups picked up these inchoate anxieties and turned them into dreamlike form. He dreamt *on behalf of* the tribe; and the dream transformed these anxious concerns into narrative form.[33] This was the beginning of a process by which Plenty Coups became entangled in the tribe's history—and in which he took on the burden of an anxious way of life. On this occasion, as a young boy, he was able to bring back to the tribe their own anxieties; only now they had the form of a story that could be told, retold—and interpreted. The elders of the tribe were then able to take the dream-narrative and turn it into an articulate, conscious thought about the challenges that the tribe would be facing.

The dream—along with the interpretation the tribe gave it—was intensely practical. Yet it was far from a straightforward application of practical reason. The dream charged young Plenty Coups—and, by extension, the tribal elders who interpreted it—to anticipate a future they did not yet know how to think about. The tribe's problem was not just that they did not know what the future had in store; they lacked the concepts with which to experience it. Their situation bears some resemblance to the pressures scientists experience before a scientific revolution.[34] Challenges build up, there is ever more pressure to explain things in the traditional ways, yet there is an inchoate sense that the old ways of explaining are leaving something unsaid. And yet one doesn't yet have the concepts with which to say it. The difference, though, is that while a scientific revolution is typically confined to an explanatory theory, the Crow faced a challenge to all aspects of their lives. Young Plenty Coups's dream was an act of *radical anticipation* in this sense: it did not merely try to predict future events; it gave the tribe imaginative tools with which to endure a conceptual onslaught. The dream told them that "a storm" was coming—but no one thought it was predicting a well-understood event like a terrible blizzard or tornado. The problem for the mid-nineteenth-century Crow was not that they lacked satellite technology and televisions. The dream-prediction was of a radically different order from anything we could learn by watching the Weather Channel. We may learn that a terrible storm is approaching and wonder whether it will be category three or whether it will reach category five. We may wonder whether the levees will hold. These are familiar questions for which we may not yet have the answers. For the recipients of Plenty Coups's dream, by contrast, the "storm" served as an enigmatic placeholder for devastation that they would understand only retrospectively—as they looked back on it in the light of concepts that had themselves been altered by the devastation. Similarly, the elders interpreted the dream to mean that if they followed the example of the chickadee, they would hold onto their lands. But what *holding onto their lands* would come to mean by say, 1955, was not something anyone could have imagined at the time of the dream, a hundred years earlier. "Holding onto our lands" at that time meant the continued ability to roam freely, in nomadic fashion, in what, from the white man's perspective, was a large but vaguely defined space around the Little Big Horn. At the time of the dream, no Crow would have envisaged that "holding onto our lands" would come to mean being confined to 2 million acres, having the property parceled out to individual owners, sold to white farmers, and so on. And yet the Crow today can proudly—and justifiably—point out that in contrast with other tribes, they were able to hold onto their lands. (I shall discuss this further in the next chapter.) And though the Crow elders at the time of the dream could not foresee this outcome, the fact that they took themselves to be going forward in the light of a dream-vision meant that they were aware that they were projecting themselves into an enigmatic future.

### The Virtue of the Chickadee

Young Plenty Coups's dream calls on him, and it gives him ethical advice—advice that seems designed to help him survive the cataclysmic rupture that is about to occur: *become a chickadee!* "He is least in strength but strongest of mind among his kind. He is willing to work for wisdom. The Chickadee-person is a good listener. Nothing escapes his ears, which he has sharpened by constant use. Whenever others are talking together of their successes and failures, there you will find the Chickadee-person listening to their words." Becoming a chickadee, then, is a virtue—a form of human excellence. One trains oneself by sharpening one's ears; one acquires the ability to learn from the wisdom of others. And after one acquires this character trait, a new form of excellence opens up: one can survive the coming storm. "The lodges of countless Bird-people were in the forest when the Four Winds charged it. Only one is left unharmed, the lodge of the Chickadee-person."[35]

Chickadee virtue called for a new form of courage, yet it drew on the traditional resources of Crow culture to do so. "The chickadee is big medicine," Pretty Shield told her interviewer. The chickadees were known by the Crow to call out which month of the winter they were in. And they were thought to be especially powerful. A chickadee once told Pretty Shield's grandmother when she was a young woman that "there is great power in little things." And the Crow well knew that offending a chickadee led to a bad outcome. The chickadee told Pretty Shield's grandmother never to eat eggs—but her husband and two of her sons refused to follow this advice, and they were all killed by the Sioux. Only one of her sons survived, just as the chickadee had predicted.[36]

So the chickadee had an established position in traditional Crow life; but in Plenty Coups's dream the chickadee was put to a new use. Young Plenty Coups was told to acquire the skills of listening and learning from others. But there was no longer any indication of what doing this might mean. In ordinary circumstances the meaning would be straightforward: if one were already in a warrior culture, one might be able to pick up tips from others about military strategy, how to shoot a bow, and so on. If one were already in a farming culture, one might pick up tips from one's neighbors about how to rotate crops, what kind of fertilizer is good for this soil, and so on. But the dream-advice to become a chickadee is being given in full recognition that upcoming events will be extraordinary. There is a storm coming that will blow down all the trees but one. And nothing is said about what constitutes the wisdom of others, what their successes are, or how one should learn from them. In particular, there is no first-order advice that one should simply pick up the skills and values of the white man. Indeed, there is no first-order advice at all—unless "learning to listen" counts as first-order behavior. Part of what it is to acquire the virtue of the chickadee is to be able to spot what the "successes" and the "wisdom" of others are—and to learn from them. The wisdom of a chickadee consists in being able to recognize the genuine wisdom of others. I shall discuss in the next chapter how this might be possible, but for the moment it suffices to note that Plenty Coups used the chickadee to radicalize a second-order virtue. It may be that the chickadee will learn from the white man in the sense of acquiring his skills and values; it may also be that the chickadee will see that there are failures in what the white man takes to be his successes, and will learn from that. And it may be that the chickadee "learns from others" in ways that allow him to go forward in entirely new directions. The only substantive commitment embodied in the chickadee virtue is that if one listens and learns from others *in the right way*—even in radically different circumstances, even with the collapse of one's world—something good will come of it.

## The Transformation of Psychological Structure

It would seem that the very traits of character that make for a courageous person would place such a person in an especially disadvantaged position to make a courageous transition *out* of traditional forms of courage. The courageous Crow warrior willingly gave up his life so that his coup-stick would not be uprooted; all his training and encouragement from early youth was directed toward producing such character. It would seem that he more than most would have found it difficult, if not impossible, to uproot what he had learned about courage.

This is a problem that philosophical studies of the virtues have tended to ignore. For we rightly think that the virtue of courage requires a certain psychological flexibility. A courageous person must know how to act well in all sorts of circumstances. We recognize that there can be times in life when the stock images of courage will be inappropriate, and the truly courageous person will recognize this extraordinary situation and act in an unusual yet courageous way. But this kind of readiness does not fully address the problem at hand. If we think of the virtues, or human excellences, as they are actually taught by cultures across history, it is plausible to expect that the virtuous person will be ready to tackle the wide variety of challenges that life might throw his way. It is unclear that there is anything in such training that will prepare him for the breakdown of the form of life itself. We would like our ethics to be grounded in psychological reality. Thus whatever flexibility is required of a virtuous person, it ought to be something that can be inculcated in the education and training of a culture. But a culture does not tend to train the young to endure its own breakdown—and it is fairly easy to see why. A culture embodies a sense of life's possibilities, and it tries to instill that sense in the young. An outstanding young member of the culture will learn to face these possibilities well. The situation we are dealing with here, however, is the breakdown of a culture's sense of possibility itself.

This inability to conceive of its own devastation will tend to be the blind spot of any culture. By and large a culture will not teach its young: "These are ways in which you can succeed, and these are ways in which you will fail; these are dangers you might face, and here are opportunities; these acts are shameful, and these are worthy of honor—and, oh yes, one more thing, this entire structure of evaluating the world might cease to make sense." This is not an impossible thought to teach, but it is a relatively new idea in the history of cultures, and one can see why a robust culture would avoid it. A culture tends to propagate itself, and it will do that by instilling its own sense of possibility in the young. If we consider the traditional training of young Crow boys, for example, it would have seemed counterproductive to teach them: "These are the ways you stand fast in front of the Sioux enemy—unless, of course, fighting becomes irrelevant, in which case we'll all have to come up with a different way of life." The first part of this lesson—which was the traditional training in courage—would seem to be undermined by the second part.

One way to focus this problem is to consider the internal, psychological dynamics of the courageous person. Courage requires that one be able to regulate a sense of honor and shame. In a traditional community like the Crow, the standards of honor and shame were rooted in the community's values—and in ritual practices of ridicule and honor. In terms of ridicule, it was typical for a person from one's father's clan to be assigned as one's personal joker. "In contrast to his own clan, whose function it is to shield him from social obloquy, the joking-relatives deliberately try to make a man ashamed by publicly jeering him and twitting him with his improper conduct."[37] This is a kind of ridicule-police; and they were used to keep people within the realm of acceptable behavior. "In the pre-reservation days," Joseph Medicine Crow reports, "the main form of Crow Indian humor was the singing of jesting songs." The rival clans would compose songs ridiculing each other for breaking tribal taboos, and for falling short in all sorts of ways.[38]

By the time a courageous person emerges in the society, the standards of courage have become standards of *self*-regulation. The courageous Crow warrior didn't avoid shameful acts because he was afraid of getting caught and shamed by his fellow tribesman. He avoided them because they were shameful. Part of what it is to be a courageous person is to have an internal sense of what is shameful—and to rule out such acts as impossible. That is, one needs good judgment about which acts are fine and which are disgraceful. In philosophical terms, one needs to be tracking shame; but one also needs to be internally motivated to turn one's back on the shameful. This is one's second nature: the ability to recognize the shameful, find it repulsive, and rule it out as impossible helps to constitute what it is to be a courageous person.

This capacity is the outcome training. The joking-relative was just one part of the training by which the Crow instilled in their children their own internal sense of what was shameful and their own internal motivation to avoid it.[39] Such an achievement requires the development of psychological structure. That is, certain psychological formations and representations in the mind can take on certain regular functions and roles. As Bernard Williams points out: "Even if shame and its motivations always involve in some way or other an idea of the gaze of another, it is important that for many of its operations the imagined gaze of an imagined other will do."[40] So, for instance, a young Crow might internalize his joking-relative: he imagines this person when he is about to perform a questionable act. He now no longer needs the prospect of actually being teased to regulate his behavior. And he does not inhibit himself because he might actually get caught. In a sense, he has already been caught—by his imagination. He is regulating himself by an internal sense of shame. This self-regulation may be conscious: one may explicitly imagine what one's mother or father would think; or one may hear an internal voice that, on reflection, one associates with a parent; or one may dream of being under the gaze of another. But nothing so explicitly conscious need occur. The point is that one has acquired a capacity for self-regulation by monitoring one's acts in relation to an internal judge. Freud called this internalized other an *ego-ideal*.[41] It is an internalization of ideals that we aspire to live up to; and when we fall too short, we experience shame.

There are three significant aspects of this developmental process. First, this imagined gaze of an imagined other is not simply a piece of imaginative content; it is performing a structural function. A person will intuit that a prospective act will evoke an experience of shame and will thereby avoid it. Second, the process by which a person acquires this sense of shame is not something he will be fully aware of. Third, once formed this structure is fairly durable. The identity and the outlook of this internalized other may change over time, but in general such changes are slow, depend on fortuitous circumstances, and are not subject to a person's will.

Plenty Coups's problem was that he developed just such a psychological structure that helped him avoid shameful acts and pursue brave ones, but he did so in the context of a world that was breaking down. If he had an ego-ideal in relation to whose gaze he felt shame, it would seem to have been an other who represented a world that—in his lifetime—ceased to exist. Perhaps it began with his joking-relative; perhaps this internal figure developed over time as young Plenty Coups learned from the brave deeds of older chiefs. We don't know precisely who his role models were, but it is clear that they were inhabitants of what was soon to become a bygone world. And once that world has collapsed, what should one make of an internalized other who continues to represent it? If his internalized other were to look down on him with a gaze full of recrimination, so what? That is, the psychological outcome would be that he felt shame—but what would be the legitimacy of this reaction? I shall address this question in detail in the next chapter.

But even now we can see that the mere fact that Plenty Coups continued to experience shame at the prospect of certain acts might show only that he was stuck in a past world, psychologically unable to face the radically new circumstances that confronted him. After all, how is one to change one's second nature? By way of comparison, consider Ajax of Sophocles' play. Athena cast a spell over Ajax so that when he thought he was killing Greek warriors, he was in fact slaughtering sheep. Only after the deed were his eyes opened to it; and in his shame he commits to suicide: "Now I am going where my way *must* go."[42] As Williams explains,

> He could not go on living . . . It was in virtue of the relations between what he expected of the world and what the world expects of a man who expects that of it. "The world" there is represented in him by an internalized other, and it is not merely any other; he would be as unimpressed by the contempt of some people as he would be by the reassurances of others. But the other in him does represent a real world, in which he would have to live if he went on living.[43]

And Williams quotes the lines of Sophocles that give insight into who his "internalized other" is:

> What countenance can I show my father Telamon?
> How will he bear the sight of me
> If I come before him naked, without any glory,

When he himself had a great crown of men's praise?
It is not something to be borne.[44]

Ajax differs from Plenty Coups in a crucial respect: the world of
the Greek warrior that Ajax inhabited remained stable through
his life. That world was represented in him by an internalized
other, in this case an internal image of his father. Future life was
intolerable for him, for if he were to endure, he would do so under the imagined gaze of an imagined other he respects who cannot possibly respect what he has done. This is the psychological
basis of Ajax's necessity: it is why he *must* go.

But let us consider a modern-day Ajax. There is no Athena
to confuse his vision. Rather, his own psychological structure
plays a similar role: it remains constant while the word around
him changes out of recognition. Imagine an Ajax who keeps on
slaughtering men and never kills a single sheep. At some point
his acts become ridiculous because the world of the Greek warrior has come to an end, but he keeps on going. This is the kind
of challenge Plenty Coups faced. If his psychological structure
had frozen him in a world in which he had to keep on planting coup-sticks, he would eventually have become ridiculous. It
would have been as though he were attacking sheep. In such a
horrible scenario it would be precisely Plenty Coups's internal
mechanisms for avoiding shame that led him into this absurd situation. This would have been a tragedy of its own.

If there are genuinely courageous ways to face a reality in
which the old forms of courage have to give way, this must involve a process by which psychological structure is altered. One
needs to transform the mechanism by which one experiences
shame. And, if one is to be truly courageous, one needs to do so

in such a way that one continues to experience shame *on the right occasions, and in the right sort of way.* It is far from clear what this kind of activity could be or how it could come about. One particular difficulty is the sense of psychological necessity that the courageous person embodies. When a courageous person sees that a certain act would be shameful, he thereby rules it out as impossible (for himself). But when a civilization collapses, there are likely to be types of act which if performed in the old world would have been shameful but which in these radically new circumstances ought not to count as shameful. For instance, in the old world it would have counted as shameful—*out of the question*—simply to abandon the prospect of stealing horses from the Sioux. In the old world this was a paradigm of counting coups. How could one give up on it now and feel no shame about it? How could anyone succeed at such a task—especially since one's psychological structure is not under the direct control of one's will?

WHAT PLENTY COUPS seems to have done is to go off into nature and dream. Let us go back to his dream and consider it not just in terms of its prophetic content but from the perspective of developing psychological structure. In the dream, Plenty Coups was visited by a Buffalo-bull person who turned into a Man-person. It was this Man-person who pointed out to him the radically new future he would have to face. The Man was a teacher-figure, who exposed Plenty Coups to a new world and asked him whether he understood it. Whatever the ultimate spiritual source of this Man-person, we need to think of him as one of Plenty Coups's internalized others. This was a creature in Plenty

Coups's imaginative world who commanded authority for him and who gave him advice. It was a voice and vision he respected. And the Man taught openness to and acceptance of the destruction of young Plenty Coups's familiar world.

The Man-person gave specific though enigmatic advice: *listen to the Chickadee-person!* The Chickadee-person has that special capacity to listen to others and to learn from them. "He is willing to work for wisdom." He is thus the bird-philosopher—in the sense that Plato gave that term: he knows that he lacks wisdom, but he yearns for it; and thus he is led to seek it from others.[45] In psychological terms, the internal figure of the Man-person instructed the young dreaming Plenty Coups to cultivate the development of the Chickadee-person as a new, but crucial, ego-ideal. Suppose young Plenty Coups were to succeed at this imaginative task. Then he would have an internalized other under whose gaze he would never feel shame when learning from others. Indeed, it would be an ego-ideal who would be encouraging him to listen and never miss a chance to learn from others. Suppose, too, that in these radically disruptive circumstances courage required one to face this new culture with openness and a willingness to learn. If that were the case, then young Plenty Coups would have dreamed himself into the new virtue of courage. And he would have done so using a traditional icon, the chickadee.

Apparently, Plenty Coups did not tell Linderman everything that happened to him that day. After young Plenty Coups had chopped off a piece of his finger, he told Linderman: "Four war-eagles were sitting in a row along a trail of my blood just above me. But they did not speak to me, offered nothing at all."[46] But from other accounts it seems that Plenty Coups was actually visited by the golden eagle, who offered him his power. As historian Timothy McCleary reports:

Why Plenty Coups did not wish to discuss this power
with Linderman is now lost to time. Nonetheless, it is
known that he had the lifelong assistance of golden ea-
gles and that this power allowed him to succeed as a warrior and war leader. The symbol of this power was a yellow dyed eagle feather. In later years he wore such a
feather on his hat to have this helper with him at all
times. As with the chickadee, the powers of the golden
eagle served him well.[47]

We are not going to be able to solve the problem of why Plenty
Coups withheld this part of his vision-quest. But, for the purposes
of the present discussion, what matters is that Plenty Coups was
able to create a psychological world in which the traditional virtues of the war eagle and the new virtues of the chickadee could
cohabit. Birds who were not of a feather could nevertheless live
together in facing the challenges of a new world.[48]

### Radical Hope

If a dream comes from a divine source *and* it tells us that our way
of life will come to an end *and* it tells us how to survive the destruction of our traditional way of life, we should expect that there
is much about the message and much about the future that we do
not yet understand. Still, the message purports to come from an
absolute source; and that kind of authority could conceivably provide something to hold onto in the face of overwhelming challenge. The Crow were told that their traditional way of life was
about to collapse. This message must have put incalculable pres-

sure on ethical life. Think of Crow ethical life as expressed in the norms and values about how to live a good life, in their ceremonial customs and established social roles, above all in their shared conception of what it was to be excellent at living a Crow life.

Plenty Coups's dream could have been seen as a divine call for a suspension of traditional ethical life. In order to survive—and perhaps to flourish again—the Crow had to be willing to give up almost everything they understand about the good life. This was not a choice that could be reasoned about in the preexisting terms of the good life. One needed some conception of—or commitment to—a goodness that transcended one's current understanding of the good. Kierkegaard coined the phrase "teleological suspension of the ethical" to describe Abraham's response to God's alleged command that he sacrifice his son.[49] That is, the ethical requirement to nurture one's children is to be suspended in the light of a higher call. What is so striking about Plenty Coups's situation is that it was a nonmythical, realistic, and plausible account of someone who experienced himself as receiving a divine call to tolerate the collapse of ethical life. This would include even a *collapse of the concepts* with which ethical life had hitherto been understood.

Obviously, we do not know precisely what happened with Plenty Coups and the Crow elders in their decision-making process. But Plenty Coups's dream gave him the resources to reason as follows:

1. My dream tells us all that our traditional way of life is coming to an end. It has been so interpreted by the wisest men of the tribe—and the tribe as a whole agrees that this is its meaning. There is nothing we can do to change that.

2.  Our conception of goods is intimately tied up with our way of life. We understand what is good in terms of our understanding of what it is to live a good life. But that is a nomadic life of hunting plentiful buffalo—and that life is about to disappear.

Thus

3.  I recognize that in an important sense we do not know what to hope for or what to aim for. Things are going to change in ways beyond which we can currently imagine. We certainly do know that we cannot face the future in the same way that we have been doing. It is no longer a matter of planning another buffalo hunt or another raid on the Sioux. We must do what we can to open our imaginations up to a radically different set of future possibilities.

Still,

4.  There is more to hope for than mere biological survival. It is not enough for me simply to survive. Another person might say, "All I care about is survival: and when I get to the other side of the abyss there will be different goods, and I'll then want them." But that is not enough for me. If everything I care about, if everything I understand as valuable, if everything I understand about myself as valuable and making life worth living—if all that is going to evaporate, I would prefer to go down in a blaze of glory. I would prefer to be a martyr to that way of life. If I am going to go on living, I need to be able to see a genuine, positive, and honorable way of going forward. So, on the one hand, I need to recognize the discontinuity that is

upon me—like it or not there will be a radical shift in form of life. On the other, I need to preserve some integrity across that discontinuity. There are some outcomes that would be worse than death. But I do have reason to hope for a dignified passage across this abyss, because

5. God—*Ah-badt-dadt-deah*—is good. My commitment to the genuine transcendence of God is manifest in my commitment to the goodness of the world transcending our necessarily limited attempt to understand it. My commitment to God's transcendence and goodness is manifested in my commitment to the idea that something good will emerge even if it outstrips my present limited capacity for understanding what that good is.

6. I am thus committed to the idea that while we Crow must abandon the goods associated with our way of life—and thus we must abandon the conception of the good life that our tribe has worked out over centuries. *We shall get the good back*, though at the moment we can have no more than a glimmer of what that might mean.

So *might* Plenty Coups have thought. Of course, we do not know what he actually thought; but this represents a remarkable movement of practical reason for which he did have the imaginative resources and which is compatible with his actions. This reasoning acknowledges that one is at some kind of practical horizon *without* thereby trying to peek over it. It is willing to reason into the future while at the same time admitting that it has no real conception of goods to work with. It is committed to the bare idea *that something good will emerge*. But it does so in recognition that one's thick understandings of the good life are about to disappear. It thereby manifests a commitment to the idea that the goodness of the world transcends one's limited and vulnerable attempts to understand it. There is no implication that one can glimpse what lies beyond the horizons of one's historically situated understanding. There is no claim to grasp ineffable truths. Indeed, this form of commitment is impressive in part because it acknowledges that no such grasp is possible. Even so, this form of reasoning shows that a very peculiar form of commitment is possible and intelligible: namely, that although Plenty Coups can recognize that his understanding of self and world is based on a set of living commitments that are vulnerable, it is nevertheless possible to commit to a goodness which transcends that understanding. He need not claim thereby to have any grasp of what that is. It is a commitment to a goodness that transcends his understanding.

In an age when secular readers often think that religious commitment breeds arrogant intolerance—as though the believers had a "direct line to God"—it is worth noting that Plenty Coups's form of commitment—at least, as we have imagined him reasoning—would lead him toward humility. He has to admit that he has little idea of what is coming—other than a "tremendous storm" that will knock down all the trees but one. The dream did not even explicitly predict that the Crow will survive—though that is how the elders interpreted it. In this way, Plenty Coups can both bear witness to the end of a traditional way of life and commit himself to a good that transcends these finite ethical forms. Precisely because Plenty Coups sees that a traditional way of life is coming to an end, he is in a position to embrace a peculiar form of hopefulness. It is basically the hope for *revival*: for coming back to life in a form that is not yet intelligible.

It is difficult to grasp the radical and strange nature of this commitment. For, on the one hand, Plenty Coups is witnessing the death of a traditional way of life. It is the death of the possibility of forming oneself as a Crow subject—at least, as traditionally understood. On the other hand, he is committed to the idea that by "listening as the Chickadee listens" he and the Crow will somehow survive. What could this mean? We would have to understand the Crow as somehow transcending their own subjectivity. That is, we would have to understand them as surviving the demise of the established ways of constituting oneself as a Crow subject. In that sense, it is no longer possible to be a Crow. And yet somehow the Crow will survive their own death. Obviously, as we have seen, the Crow have survived, biologically speaking; they have survived as a social group. But these meager forms of survival do not constitute the full flower of Plenty Coups's hope. He is committed to some more robust form of flourishing than that. And yet, precisely because he is witness to the death of traditional Crow subjectivity, he is not in a position to say what the future form of Crow flourishing will be. Still, on the basis of his dream, he commits himself to the idea that—on the other side of the abyss—the Crow shall survive, perhaps flourish again. *The Crow is dead, long live the Crow!* This is a form of hope that seems to survive the destruction of a way of life. Though it must be incredibly difficult to hold onto this commitment in the midst of subjective catastrophe, it is not impossible. And it is at least conceivable that this is just what Plenty Coups did.

Commitment to this possibility in no way commits one to the idea that the world is the expression of a theodicy. Nor does it commit one to the wildly politically incorrect view that western civilization is a higher form; that the Crow would be better off to adapt to it. It would have been possible for Plenty Coups to commit to his dream and still view the onset of western civilization as a disaster. It would have been possible for him to commit to a good that transcends his current conception and still hope that the Crow will reemerge as a radical alternative to white culture. The commitment is not to the idea that history has a beneficial direction, nor to the idea that its current order has divine sanction. After all, in the possibility being explored in these pages, Plenty Coups has declared that history has come to an end. Rather, the commitment is only to the bare possibility that, from this disaster, something good will emerge: the Crow shall somehow survive. Why that will be or how that will be is left open. The hope is held in the face of the recognition that, given the abyss, one cannot really know what survival means.

From the perspective of this commitment, the rebellion of Wraps His Tail isn't just futile; it is a nostalgic evasion. Wraps His Tail correctly saw that the traditional Crow way of life was under threat. And he correctly saw that *if* he was to defend that traditional way of life, he must plant his coup-stick. He must count coups. Any other form of defense would itself be a break with tradition—and this, for him, was impossible. For him, *there was no other way for a Crow* to go forward. And in some sense he was right. Crow excellence—and thus the possibility of forming oneself as a Crow subject—was expressed in a world of living possibilities. He took up a position in that world that he had to occupy: the position of a Crow warrior. Or at least, he attempted to take up such a position. The problem was that the world was collapsing around him. Wraps His Tail tried to hold onto this position in spite of the fact that it became unintelligible. Plenty Coups's position, by contrast, was ironic: the only way for a Crow to go forward was to acknowledge that the traditional way of life was going to be blown away in a storm. Only after the storm would new Crow possibilities open up. That was the form of Plenty Coups's commitment: to the possibility of new Crow possibilities. Even though the Crow have to give up a way of life—and thus give up the subjectivity entangled in that way of life—the Crow shall nevertheless survive. But what this means—at least at the time of the dream and its interpretation—cannot be fully understood.

And though, for the Crow, this dream-advice had divine sanction, there was no guarantee that even the conception of divinity would remain stable. Perhaps even the conception of God would change in ways that—at the time of the dream—were unimaginable. Plenty Coups would probably have had to hold onto the idea that his dream was somehow a source of truth, but little else in his outlook had to remain constant. We know, for instance, that as a grown man, Plenty Coups negotiated with the Catholic missionaries to found a school near his home in Pryor so that the children of his clan would not have to go to the school at Crow Agency, sixty miles away.[50] He himself was baptized and married in the church. And, looking to a future that Plenty Coups could not have imagined, in 2005 the Crow hip-hop group Reza-wrecktion won the Native American Music Award in Los Angeles.[51] The dream gained its authority via divine sanction; but the exact nature of this divine source—as well as what kinds of narratives and rituals were appropriate to it—was also left open. All the Crow needed—minimally speaking—was a sense that the dream provided a legitimate source of guidance. And they needed to be able to hold onto that sense of legitimacy as they weathered the storm. Doing so would provide them with the resources to commit to the bare idea that after the storm there would be something good *for them*.

Finding a way to flourish is the task for a new gen
Crow. Plenty Coups himself became a farmer, and h
aged others to do the same. Other Crow have becon
and have been successful fighting to protect Crow ir
court. Perhaps there will be room for a new interpretatio
it is to lay down a coup-stick. Or perhaps the coup-s
its metaphorical derivatives—will become irrelevant. C
historian has argued that the Crow were originally a
tribe, and that their nomadic, hunting period represe
riod of separation from their origins. In returning to fari
Crow would thus not be following the white example so
returning to their ancient origins. As Barney Old Coyote
the *Encyclopedia of North American Indians*,

> The Crows began as an agricultural and quasi-sedent;
> tribe. They became a nomadic, hunting tribe, and toc
> they constitute a rural community occupying a federa
> Indian reservation, but with members both on and off
> the reservation. Until the 1930s the majority of tribal
> members spoke only the Crow language, but today the
> majority speak English. Contemporary life-styles and
> mores are intermeshed with ancient Crow culture, tra(
> tion, and systems of worship.[52]

In another imaginable narrative, the Crow would agai
ish by embracing American values. In another, they would
ward in new ways that would teach the American people v;
lessons. How the Crow should go forward it is not my busi
say. I am only pointing out the radical form of hopefulne
bedded in Plenty Coups's vision: that even with the death
traditional forms of Crow subjectivity, the Crow can never
survive—and flourish again.

Plenty Coups was able to lead himself and his people forward into an unimaginable future committed to the idea that something good would emerge. He carried himself and his people forward, committed to the idea that it was worthwhile to do so, even while acknowledging that his own local understanding of the good life would vanish. This is a daunting form of commitment: to a goodness in the world that transcends one's current ability to grasp what it is. We do not know the depths of Plenty Coups's thought. He may have engaged in a shallow form of instrumental reasoning; he may have had profound insight into history; he may have expressed religious conviction as he tried to help his people hold onto their promised land. The historical evidence is compatible with all these interpretations—and others. And yet all these interpretations manifest a bedrock of hope. There may be various forms of ethical criticism one might be tempted to level at this form of hopefulness: that it was too complacent; that it didn't face up to the evil that had been inflicted on the Crow tribe. But it is beyond question that the hope was a remarkable human accomplishment—in no small part because it avoided despair. What we are to think about that is the topic of the next chapter.

# III

## CRITIQUE OF ABYSMAL

## REASONING

### *The Legitimacy of Radical Hope*

FOR WHAT MAY we hope? Kant put this question in the first-person singular along with two others—What can I know? and What ought I to do?—that he thought essentially marked the human condition.[1] With two centuries of philosophical reflection, it seems that these questions are best transposed to the first-person plural. And with that same hindsight: rather than attempt an a priori inquiry, I would like to consider hope as it might arise at one of the limits of human existence. In the scenario outlined in the preceding chapter, Plenty Coups responded to the collapse of his civilization with radical hope. What makes this hope *radical* is that it is directed toward a future goodness that transcends the current ability to understand what it is. Radical hope anticipates a good for which those who have the hope as yet lack the appropriate concepts with which to understand it. What would it be for such hope to be justified?

In the preceding chapter I hypothesized that young Plenty Coups dreamt on behalf of his tribe. The tribe was anxious—indeed, a way of life was anxious about its own ability to endure. Through the interpretation of the dream the tribe surmised that the traditional ways of life—and thus the traditional ways of being a Crow—were coming to an end. And yet they gathered confidence that they would survive. In this way, the Crow hoped for the emergence of a Crow subjectivity that did not yet exist. There would be ways of continuing to form oneself as a Crow subject— ways to flourish as a Crow—even though the traditional forms were doomed. This hope is radical in that it is aiming for a subjectivity that is at once Crow and does not yet exist.

Again, the point is not to establish the historical claim that Plenty Coups actually did manifest such radical hope. I suspect he did—and the historical record is consistent with this hypothesis—but I am not in a position to plumb the depths of his soul. Nor thus is the aim to defend Plenty Coups. The aim is to establish what *we* might legitimately hope at a time when the sense of purpose and meaning that has been bequeathed to us by our culture has collapsed. And thus the central question for us is not: Was Plenty Coups justified in his hope? but rather: What would it have been for Plenty Coups to have been justified? This is a way in which a historical example might contribute to a distinctively philosophical reflection. If anything is going to answer to the name *moral psychology*, it ought to be an inquiry into how the formations (and transformations) of the psyche help one to lead a good life in a world with others.[2] An actual historical example— as well as an imaginative construction built on concrete historical circumstances—can provide the needed texture for an informative moral-psychological inquiry. We can learn from Plenty Coups: not about him so much as about ourselves. And we can learn from him not because he has some special alternative wisdom that the western mind lacks—this is a distinctively western trope adopted in relation to "the Indian"[3]—but because he is an exemplary human being living through an extraordinary time. He actually did live through a collapse of civilization, and in the face of that onslaught he led his people. He may thus help us to better understand one of life's remoter but significant possibilities.

For Plenty Coups the question of hope was intimately bound to the question of how to live. Because he took his hope to be justified, he chose to live—and to lead the Crow—in distinctive ways. Thus the issue of hope becomes crucial for an ethical inquiry into life at the horizons of one's understanding. And this gives us a clue as to how we might formulate an investigation into the legitimacy of hope. For, after all, it would seem that it is not always to be said in favor of a person that he lived with hope. We use the term "Pollyanna" pejoratively to designate someone whose hopefulness depends on averting her gaze from devastating reality. Indeed, we sometimes suspect that a person's hopefulness is a strategy for averting her gaze. This may be a psychologically effective strategy for coping with awful circumstances—and we may thus sympathize—but we don't think of it as fine or admirable. And, of course, there is a special danger for anyone who makes the kind of decision Plenty Coups made. In the face of an onslaught by a dominant civilization, Plenty Coups decided to collaborate with it. In certain historical circumstances, we use the term "collaboration" pejoratively to designate a craven capitulation to an evil dominant force (as when describing those who collaborated with the Nazis in World War II). In such circumstances, one's hope can be used in the service of self-deception: one avoids seeing the cravenness of one's acts because one takes oneself to be ushering in a hopeful future.

This is the challenge that Chief Sitting Bull laid down. Sitting

Bull was the last great chief of the Sioux Nation (the Lakota tribes), the traditional enemy of the Crow. He is best known for being the principal chief at the time the Sioux inflicted their legendary defeat on the U.S. Seventh Cavalry under General George Custer in June 1876. About a decade later, in September 1886—after he first fled to Canada, then returned and surrendered to U.S. forces and was placed on the Sioux reservation—Sitting Bull made a visit to the Crow reservation. He stayed for two weeks.[4] It would be difficult to exaggerate the historical novelty of this occasion. Here were two traditional enemies—who had slaughtered each other in recurrent waves for over a century—coming together to talk things over in the wake of radical historical change. He visited the battlefield at Little Big Horn, where there was now a monument to Custer; but he drew the opposite lesson from that intended by those who erected it.

> The charismatic old warrior turned to his hosts after viewing the Seventh Cavalry's resting place and declared, "Look at that monument. That marks the work of our people: See how the white men treat us and how they treat you. We get one and one half pounds of beef per ration, while you receive but one half pound. You are kept at home and made to work like slaves, while we do not labor and are permitted to ride from agency to agency and enjoy ourselves."[5]

Above all: "Sitting Bull insisted that authentic tribal leaders would never cooperate with the American government. To do so would be to surrender one's personal authority and sacrifice one's followers to the whims of petty officials."[6]

In effect, Sitting Bull impugned Plenty Coups's judgment and leadership. And insofar as radical hope played a role, he impugned that, too. Sitting Bull was a traditional enemy of the Crow; so there is some question of how much pain he still wanted to inflict upon them. Perhaps he wanted to brag at their expense. And he had been a formidable enemy of the U.S. government; so there is also a question of whether he wanted to continue to stir up trouble for them. Perhaps he wished to disrupt the Crow foreign policy and get them to fight against the Americans. To some extent he succeeded. His visit seems to have played a role in stirring up the discontent that led to Wraps His Tail's rebellion.[7] Obviously, we cannot know what motivated Sitting Bull to make his case. But if we take him at face value—as some of the Crow did—he impugned Plenty Coups's judgment. From Sitting Bull's perspective, Plenty Coups was a gullible sap or, worse, a collaborator with malign forces.[8] Either way he exercised poor judgment.

But this objection points the way to a possible vindication of radical hope. One response to Sitting Bull would be to argue that, on the contrary, Plenty Coups exercised excellent judgment and courageous leadership. To promote that position, one would need to argue that even in such extreme circumstances certain forms of human excellence are still possible. And rather than arguing for radical hope in isolation, one would argue that such hope may play a crucial role in a courageous life. Thus we are led to an investigation of what courage might be in such challenging times. If we can persuade ourselves that even in these extreme circumstances courage is a genuine virtue—that is, a state of character whose exercise contributes to the living of an excellent life—then if we can also show that radical hope is an important ingredient of such courage, we have thereby provided a legitimation of such hope.

Clearly, both Sitting Bull and Plenty Coups were men of extraordinary dignity and ability; both were struggling to figure out an honorable way for their people to live; and both deserve our respect. But if we are to vindicate radical hope in the way in which I think it can be vindicated, we must see Plenty Coups as embodying a form of courage that Sitting Bull did not grasp. History had rendered the traditional, thick understanding of courage impossible—indeed, it had drained it of meaning. But this outcome did not mean that courage as a human excellence had become impossible. Even in this cultural devastation there were ways to live a worthwhile and important human life—and courage would be an essential virtue. But courage had to undergo a transformation: in particular, there had to be a *thinning out* of what had been a thick concept. Plenty Coups had to come to understand courage in terms that transcended counting coups. In this chapter I want to explore the role that radical hope might have played in thinning out the virtue of courage.

### Aristotle's Method

For Aristotle, the virtues are states of character the exercise of which contributes to living an excellent life. He did not confront the problem that different historical epochs might impose different requirements on what states of the soul could count as courage. And thus the conception of courage I shall explore here extends beyond the virtue that Aristotle explicitly considered. Nevertheless, his method gives us the tools with which we might pursue this inquiry. Aristotle thought of virtue as an intermediate state of the soul, existing between other psychic formations which—in the light of that virtue—can be seen as excesses or deficiencies. The important point for our inquiry is that we come to understand what courage is, in part, by differentiating it from what it is not. Courage, for Aristotle, lies in a mean between cowardice, which is a deficiency, and rash boldness, which is an excess.[9] In the situation under consideration the deficiency might be a craven capitulation to the dominant culture—which is what Sitting Bull alleged—and the excess might be the rash and ineffectual rebellion that Wraps His Tail instigated. One can allow the content of courage to shift while nevertheless continuing to locate it in a matrix of excess and defect.

And Aristotle supplies us with broad-scale hallmarks of courage, in relation to which we can track its changes. That is, even if courage began as a paradigmatically military virtue—as it did for the ancient Greeks, as it did for the Crow—it might have more general marks and features that would allow for a thinning out of the virtue. If the world shifts, there may be concomitant shifts in what can count as courageous, but for anything to count as courage, it must fall within this framework. I want to isolate five criteria that Aristotle gives us that together set out the field in which courage must lie.

*1. A courageous person has a proper orientation toward what is shameful and what is fearful.*[10]

That is, he grasps what would be truly shameful and he is thereby motivated to avoid it. He also understands what is genuinely fearful—"No one is better at understanding what is frightening"—

and yet he is nevertheless motivated to act courageously in the face of it. With cultural devastation such as the Crow endured, a courageous person would have had to reorient himself to the shameful and the fearful. Aristotle says that the courageous person is generally thought to be a person who is fearless about a fine death.[11] For centuries the Crow understood this requirement in terms of planting a coup-stick and counting coups. For the Crow, these were quintessential manifestations of the fearlessness of the courageous person. And, of course, this paradigm raises the question: If Plenty Coups was courageous, why didn't he choose to go down fighting—planting his coup-stick—against a force that would deprive his people of their traditional way of life? If we are to adhere to this Aristotelian criterion, the answer must take the form: Because Plenty Coups *correctly* saw that dying in such a way would no longer be a fine death; and thus avoiding such a death should no longer count as shameful.

This brings us to the second hallmark of courage:

### 2. *Courage aims toward what is fine.*[12]

Aristotle points out that people can perform courageous acts and yet not be courageous when the act flows from the wrong sort of motivation. Thus a person might act appropriately and boldly— but do so from peer pressure. Similarly, a cornered animal may fight boldly for survival—but it is acting from instinct. "Human beings too, then, are distressed when angry and take pleasure in retaliating; but people who fight from these motives are effective in fighting, not courageous, since they do not fight because of what is fine or noble, or as correct prescription directs, but from emotion."[13] Thus for Plenty Coups's acts to qualify as courageous, we must see him as doing more than fighting for his own survival. We must see him as doing so because he is aiming for something fine.

> 3. *A courageous person must grasp the situation he or she is in and, through experience, exercise good judgment.*[14]

I shall call this exercise of good judgment *facing up to reality*. In the militaristic paradigm, the courageous soldier has a good idea—acquired from experience—of what constitutes a real military danger and what does not. Because he is able to assess the situation accurately, he is in the best position to inflict damage on the enemy, avoid defeat, and win where possible. This, says Aristotle, is why Socrates thought that courage was a kind of expert knowledge.[15] As we shall see, it was possible for the Crow to hold onto this warrior paradigm even after their way of life had shifted. But for Plenty Coups's acts to count as courageous, they had to flow from an accurate understanding that the situation had so fundamentally changed that the requirements of courage had to change along with them.

> 4. *Courage paradigmatically involves the risk of serious loss and of enduring certain pains.*[16]

Again, for Aristotle as well as for the nomadic Crow, the paradigm is war: the courageous person risks death and endures hardship for the sake of what is fine. He grasps that there are fates worse than death and pleasures not worth having, because they are shameful. In a period of cultural devastation such as Plenty Coups and the Crow had to endure, there would have to be a radical transformation in the risks associated with courage. At such a historical moment, traditional examples of risk—counting coups—have become weirdly irrelevant. And the risks that do arise are of a different order: the risks of facing a future that one as yet lacks concepts to understand. Are there courageous ways of facing a future for which the traditional conception of courage has become inapplicable?

This is not a question that Aristotle ever asked; and one can see that it has distinctive challenges. In a robust culture a courageous person will take risks, but he will have an established framework for understanding what those risks are. And it is in terms of that framework that he will develop an excellent capacity for risk-assessment and the ability to act well in the light of those risks. But at a time of cultural collapse, the courageous person has, as it were, to take a risk on the framework itself. Plenty Coups had to risk inadvertently taking himself and his people down a shameful path—at a time before the framework in which shame could be evaluated was firmly established. The old standards for assessing shame—for example, failing to plant a coup-stick—were no longer applicable, but new and adequate standards for assessing shame were not yet in place. Thus Plenty Coups had to take a risk on what would come to count as courage in these radically altered circumstances. And, as we saw in Chapter I, he had to endure hardship and pain to stick with it.

Finally, there is one negative criterion:

> 5. *Bold acts that derive merely from optimism are not themselves courageous.*[17]

They are at best a simulacrum of courage. Truly courageous people act from the motives and judgment outlined above, whereas merely confident persons are so because they just assume they are strongest and no harm will come to them.[18] This will be a central challenge: to show that Plenty Coups's acts plausibly flowed from genuine courage rather than from false optimism.

## Radical Hope versus Mere Optimism

Plenty Coups's hope is manifest in his fidelity to his prophetic dream. He never abandoned the idea that he had been given a vision that derived from the spiritual world. This was a particular form of steadfastness. It was not just that he had a significant dream; he held onto it and led the tribe in the light of it. Psychologically speaking, he no doubt used his dream to sustain hope. But ethically speaking, Plenty Coups made a claim: that if the tribe adhered to the dream they would face an inevitable devastation but they would survive. Indeed, they would come out the other side with new ways to live well. This would be the life under the auspices and example of the chickadee—*whatever that might come to mean.* Plenty Coups's claim to lead was based on a claim to be exercising good judgment in the face of radical historical change. In effect, he made a claim to an unusual form of excellence: he was the one who was able to face up to an (as yet) ungraspable reality. Thus his capacity to have that dream and to stick to its meaning is a manifestation of courage.

We do not need to agree with Plenty Coups's theory of dreams in order to see his hope as a manifestation of courage. But we would need to see his dream as somehow responsive to reality; and responsive in ways that manifest human excellence. There are basically three ways in which one might see Plenty Coups's dream as a manifestation of human excellence, two of them religious, one secular:

- Accept the Crow theory of dreams: Plenty Coups was visited by the spiritual figures who are represented in the dream.

- Agree that Plenty Coups's dream does have some spiritual basis, but assume that it was given to him in a mythical, and thus somewhat distorted, form.

- Assume that Plenty Coups's dream did not have a divine source but was rather rooted in human wishes, anxieties, and perceptions. Nevertheless one could insist that Plenty Coups was using his imaginative capacity to "hook onto" reality and track it in unusual ways.

This last position disagrees with Plenty Coups's theory of dreams but accepts that his dream-life facilitated his living a genuinely courageous life. In short, the claim would be that he was right to remain faithful to his dream; and that doing so was a manifestation of courage. In this chapter I want to make a case which is compatible with any of these options. If this book should attract a Crow reader, it is likely that he or she will believe the first option, the Crow theory of dreams. Some religious readers of other faiths might be inclined to believe the second option. But I want to show that even the secular reader who does not believe that dreams have any relation to a divine or supernatural realm might nevertheless have reason to see Plenty Coups's imaginative life as playing a crucial role in genuine courage. In a sense, the case for this third, secular, interpretation is the hardest to make. If the dream had been divine revelation, then sticking to it was obviously a human excellence. And if this divinely inspired dream were helping a person face reality well, it could arguably count as a constituent of courage. But, for the sake of this argument, I would like to put those assumptions aside. The aim of defending the secular account is to show that even an atheist has reason to accept that Plenty Coups's leadership counts as courageous. The judgment of Plenty Coups's courage does not hang on religious orientation or lack of one.

In the interpretation I am exploring, Plenty Coups had his dream in the context of a communal sense of anxiety. A way of life was anxious about its ability to go forward into an unfathomable future. The dream was a manifestation of radical hope—and it gave the tribe the resources to adopt a stance of radical hope—in that it enabled them to go forward hopefully into a future that they would be able to grasp only retrospectively, when they could reemerge with concepts with which to understand themselves and their experiences. If we can make the case that this stance was a manifestation of courage, we could presumably come to see how radical hope can be not just psychologically advantageous but a legitimate response even to a world catastrophe.

One objection that needs to be met right away derives from the work of Freud. In *The Interpretation of Dreams*, Freud argues that dreams are disguised gratifications of unconscious wishes.[19] On this view, all we can truly learn about from a dream is the nature of our own wishful longings. And insofar as we think we are learning about some independent reality, we are collaborating in a process by which we keep the wishful nature of our dreams from conscious awareness. If this was all there was to be said for dreams, then we would have to judge Plenty Coups's commitment to his dream as wish-fulfilling optimism rather than courage. For, on this account, he would mistakenly be taking himself to be facing up to reality (and thus failing the third criterion of the courageous person). Rather than getting a real glimpse into the future, he would wishfully be gratifying his own longings. And if the dream were only a wish-fulfillment, then sticking to it steadfastly through life as though it were giving him real information about the world would be a paradigm of what Freud calls "turning away from reality."[20] That is, instead of facing up to the challenges that the world presents, one stubbornly clings to a dreamlike fantasy—as a way of wishfully avoiding those challenges. If, like Aristotle, we think of virtue as lying in a mean between excess and defect, this "turning away from reality" would be a serious defect when it came to courage. It would also fail the second criterion: that the courageous person aims for the fine. For even if it happened to lead to good consequences, there is nothing particularly noble in mistaking one's own wishes for a higher cause. Indeed, one way to read this Freudian objection is as giving us a psychological account of what mere "optimism"— the fifth criterion—consists in. If Plenty Coups is only sticking to his wishes, then his leadership, however beneficial, is merely confident, not courageous.

Obviously, this Freudian line of objection needs to be resisted. And I think it can be—in part, by making use of other materials that Freud himself gave us. Freud eventually abandoned the idea that every dream was the gratification of a wish. In particular, he left open the possibility that a dream might be a manifestation— and representation—of anxiety.[21] And anxiety can be a realistic response to the world. In this way, an anxiety-dream can function as a signal of real danger. But as soon as one makes this admission, the categorical quality of the Freudian objection falls apart.

For if a dream can itself be a response to reality, it is at least possible that certain uses of this imaginative capacity might help us to respond better to the world's challenges than we would be able to do without it. And if that is so, certain capacities of imagination might actually be constituents of a courageous soul.

Furthermore, even if we grant that a certain dream has a wishful component, the existence of that component does not thereby rule it out as a manifestation of courage. By way of analogy, think of ordinary conscious action. We take such actions to be outcomes of beliefs and desires: the mere fact that certain desires are involved does not thereby render action unresponsive to reality. It may be our desires that help us focus our beliefs or shift them in imaginative ways, and thereby help us better to face the situation. As long as a dream can be an imaginative response to reality, there is going to be a question not just of *whether* wishes are expressed in it, but *how* they are expressed. In particular, there is the possibility that our wishes could be integrated into an overall functioning of our imaginative capacity in such a way as to facilitate a creative and appropriate response to the world's challenges. We thus have room for the idea of *imaginative excellence* when it comes to ethical life. This is the claim that needs to be defended on Plenty Coups's behalf: that his dream may have expressed his wishes—both for himself and for the tribe—but that it also responded to the anxiety that his tribe shared. This anxiety was itself a realistic response to the world. And the radical hope that young Plenty Coups's dream generated was itself a manifestation of imaginative excellence. It enabled the tribe to face its future courageously—*and imaginatively*—at a time when the traditional understanding of courage was becoming unlivable.

## Courage and Hope

Thus far I have argued that Plenty Coups's dream tracked reality at two levels. First, it picked up the anxiety of the tribe and responded to it. Second, insofar as the tribe's anxiety was justified—that it was a response to a menacing yet uncertain future—the dream addressed this real-life challenge at one remove. But the case for imaginative excellence can be made stronger than that.

At a time of radical historical change, the concept of courage will itself require new forms. This is the reality that needs to be faced—the *call for concepts*—and it would seem that if one were to face up to such a challenge well it would have to be done imaginatively. Courage, as a state of character, is constituted in part by certain ideals—ideals of what it is to live well, to live courageously. These ideals are alive in the community, but they also take hold in a courageous person's soul. As we saw in the preceding chapter, these ideals come to constitute a courageous person's ego-ideal.[22] In traditional times, it was in terms of such an ideal that a courageous warrior would "face up to reality"—that is, decide what to do in the face of changing circumstances. But now, "facing up to reality" seemed to include facing up to a situation in which those traditional ideals were no longer applicable. And yet, these ideals helped to constitute the courageous person's psychological structure. So if there were to be such a thing as a courageous response to these radically altered circumstances, it would seem to require a transformation of the psychological structure with which we "face up to reality." At a time of cultural devastation, the reality a courageous person has to face up to is that one has to face up to reality in new ways.

Courage thus seems to have its own vicissitudes. We are all familiar with the image of the "old-timer": a person whose ideals and outlook would have been appropriate in a previous time or culture, but who cannot or will not change with the changing times. However unfairly, such people are stuck in the past. As we have seen, it would seem that courageous people in any robust culture are especially vulnerable to this problem, for they are the ones who have deeply internalized the traditional courageous ideals. One might think that they would therefore be the least able to make the psychological changes that courage now requires. Someone might wish to argue that, on occasion, such stubborn insistence on older ideals is itself a form of courage: a courageous insistence on the importance of these ideals. In certain historical circumstances that is no doubt the case. But, following Plenty Coups, I want to inquire into the circumstances in which courage does require this internal transformation: How might it occur, and why would it count *as courage?* Let us grant that such a transformation would count as an adaptation to a new reality; but why think of that adaptation as courageous?

To answer this question, we need to take a step back and ask more generally: What is it about courage that makes it a virtue— that is, a human excellence? Courage is a virtue, I think, because it is an excellent way of coping with, responding to, and manifesting a basic fact about us: that we are finite erotic creatures. By *finite* I mean to point to a family of limitations that characterize the human condition: we are not all-powerful or all-knowing; our ability to create is limited; so is our ability to get what we want; our beliefs may be false; and even the concepts with which we understand the world are vulnerable. With the Crow, the concepts in terms of which they understood the good life became impossible ways of understanding their lives. Even when we try to think about the world we inhabit, think about ourselves and our lives, we take a risk that the very concepts with which we think may become unintelligible. By *erotic* I follow a basically Platonic conception that, in our finite condition of lack, we reach out to the world in yearning, longing, admiration, and desire for that which (however mistakenly) we take to be valuable, beautiful, and good.[23]

Thus, as finite erotic creatures it is an essential part of our nature that we take risks just by being in the world. As finite creatures we are vulnerable: we may suffer physical and emotional injury, we may make significant mistakes, even the concepts with which we understand ourselves and the world may collapse—and yet as erotic creatures we reach out to the world and try to embrace it. For all the risks involved, we make an effort to live with others; on occasion we aspire to intimacy; we try to understand the world; on occasion we try to express ourselves and create something; we aim toward living (what we take to be) a happy life. As finite, erotic creatures it is a necessary aspect of our existence that our lives are marked by risk. We are familiar with the idea that we are creatures who necessarily inhabit a world. But *a world* is not merely the environment in which we move about; it is *that over which we lack omnipotent control, that about which we may be mistaken in significant ways, that which may intrude upon us, that which may outstrip the concepts with which we seek to understand it.* Thus living within a world has inherent and unavoidable risk. If we abstract from the thick conceptions of courage that a culture may put forward in a particular historical period—

whether martial valor or counting coups or maintaining a stiff upper lip or being true to one's conscience—and ask in the most general terms what it is about courage that makes it a human excellence, the answer, I think, is that courage is the capacity for living *well* with the risks that inevitably attend human existence. At times when a culture was organized around battle—as with the nomadic Crow, as with the Homeric Greeks—courage was understood in terms of the risks of battle; at a time of, say, the Protestant Reformation in Europe, courage was conceived in terms of standing alone with one's conscience before God. In different times, in different cultures, there may be different risks; but as long as we are alive and human we will have to tolerate and take risks. The courageous person is someone who is excellent at taking those risks. That is why courage counts as a virtue: it is an excellent way of inhabiting and embracing our finite erotic nature.

Plato saw that it was a condition of our finite erotic natures that we intuit that goodness outstrips our ability to grasp it. In the *Republic*, Socrates says, "Every soul pursues the good and does whatever it does for its sake. It divines that the good is something, but it is perplexed and cannot adequately grasp what it is or acquire the sort of stable beliefs it has about other things."[24] For the purposes of the present discussion, we do not have to go along with Plato's metaphysics to see him as making an important point—one with which almost all readers will agree. We do not have to agree with Plato that there is a transcendent source of goodness—that is, a source of goodness that transcends the world—to think that the goodness *of the world* transcends our finite powers to grasp it. The emphasis here is not on some mysterious source of goodness, but on the limited nature of our finite conceptual resources. This, I think most readers will agree, is an *appropriate* response for finite creatures like ourselves. Indeed, it seems oddly inappropriate—lacking in understanding of oneself as a finite creature—to think that what is good about the world is exhausted by our current understanding of it. Even the most strenuously secular readers ought to be willing to accept this form of transcendence. And this is the core of Plenty Coups's commitment. His specifically religious beliefs were crucially important to him, but in my opinion, they gave him the sustenance with which he could hold onto this core commitment through the storm. The core commitment itself can be held by the secular and the religious; it is an appropriate response to our being finite natures.

And if that is an appropriate response, one can see how our erotic natures might lead us toward it. According to Plato and to Freud—who self-consciously followed this Platonic line of thought—we are born into the world *longingly*.[25] We instinctively reach out to parental figures for emotional and nutritional sustenance that, in the moment, we lack the resources to understand. This is the archaic prototype of radical hope: in infancy we are reaching out for sustenance from a source of goodness even though we as yet lack the concepts with which to understand what we are reaching out for. Let us leave to one side the misfires and tragedies of human upbringing and consider the case in which the parenting is "good enough."[26] And by "parenting" I do not mean merely the acts of the biological parents but all the nurturing acts of all the nurturing figures in a nurturing environment. Part of the sustenance our parenting figures will give us is the concepts with which we can at least begin to understand what we are longing *for*. This is a crucial aspect of acquiring a natural language: inheriting a culture's set of concepts through which we can understand ourselves as desiring, wishing, and hoping for certain things. It is because of our finite, erotic natures that we come to conceive of ourselves as finite erotic creatures.

We are now in a position to see how Plenty Coups's response to the challenging circumstances of his time might count as courage. First, let us abstract from all the familiar thick images of courage and consider it as the ability to live well with the risks that inevitably attend human existence. To be human is necessarily to be a vulnerable risk-taker; to be a courageous human is to be good at it. That is, a courageous person has the psychological resources to face the risks with dignity and to make good judgments in the light of them. Second, at a time of cultural devastation such as Plenty Coups faced, the risks include not only malnutrition, starvation, disease, defeat, and confinement; they include *loss of concepts*. In such circumstances, courage would have to include the ability to live well with the risk of conceptual loss. Let us, for the sake of argument, assume that in Plenty Coups's time hope for a future that could not yet be grasped was a good response to the devastation they faced. In such a way, radical hope might be not only compatible with courage: in times of radical change, it might function as a necessary constituent. Again, there might be false simulacra of courage: cases in which an insistent and unresponsive "optimism" is at work, rather than an appropriate manifestation of hope. To be a manifestation of courage, radical hope must be well deployed. Still, we begin to see how Plenty Coups's radical hope might be legitimated as a remarkably courageous response to his times.

## Virtue and Imagination

I have argued that in times of radical historical change—in particular, at times when one's culture is collapsing—there may be demands made on a courageous person that outstrip traditional training and traditional patterns of character-formation. At such times, to *remain* courageous one might have to endure or bring about significant psychological changes. One might need a kind of psychological flexibility that goes beyond anything the culture was trying to instill when it taught the flexibilities of courage. If we look to the details of Plenty Coups's dream-life, we can gain insight into how these psychological transformations might come about.

There are two significant dreams to examine. The first occurred almost a year before the prophetic dream that we considered in the preceding chapter. Young Plenty Coups's beloved older brother had gone out on a warparty against the Sioux, and he was killed. In mourning, Plenty Coups, just nine years old, climbed a nearby mountain and had a dream-vision.[27] In the dream, young Plenty Coups was taken up by the Dwarf-chief, the head of the Little People, and told that they would be a source of lifelong protection. The Little People were legendary creatures who lived in the hills and valley near Pryor, Montana, where Plenty Coups made his home in later years. The Crows believed that they had made the stone arrowheads to be found on the ground there, since all the Indians they knew made arrowheads out of bone. In effect, the Dwarf-chief blessed young Plenty Coups's own capacity for excellence:

"He will be a Chief," said the Dwarf-chief. "I can give him nothing. He already possesses the power to become great if he will use it. Let him cultivate his senses, let him use the powers which Ah-badt-dadt-deah [God] has given him, and he will go far. The difference between men grows out of the use, or non-use, of what was given them by Ah-badt-dadt-deah in the first place . . . In you as in all men are natural powers. You have a will. Learn to use it. Make it work for you. Sharpen your senses as you would sharpen your knife. Remember the wolf smells better than you do because he has learned to depend on his nose. It tells him every secret the winds carry because he uses it all the time, makes it work for him. We can give you nothing. You already possess everything necessary to become great. Use your powers. Make them work for you, and you will become a Chief."[28]

Let us leave to one side the question whether there are Little People and whether they visited Plenty Coups.[29] Psychologically speaking, the Little People function as transitional figures for young Plenty Coups: because they are taken to exist as some aspect of the spirit world, the question whether their voices come from inside or outside is left vague.[30] We can think of these voices as the voices of an emerging ego-ideal. Note that they emerge in response to a real-life loss: the loss of a beloved older brother who, if he had lived, could have guided young Plenty Coups, provided a role model, and taught him how to grow up to be a courageous Crow warrior. But what they tell him, in effect, is that he can survive that loss *and flourish*. One might think of the older brother as standing for—and embodying—the traditional Crow virtues. Note that the Dwarf-chief does not give Plenty Coups specific advice, nor does he encourage the traditional virtues per se. He does not say, "Be sure to practice with bow and arrow" or "Take the first opportunity to plant a coup-stick." Rather, he more generally encourages Plenty Coups to develop his senses and his will. He already has all it takes to become great, if only he will develop his skills. In this way, the Dwarf-chief encourages Plenty Coups to courage. And it is a form of courage that is left vague and open-ended. (In this sense the Dwarf-chief does seem a precursor of the worthy chickadee.) In effect, the Dwarf-chief tells him that if he develops his own capacities, he will develop the ability to meet the world's challenges with skill and wisdom. This is a voice of hope that can play a significant role in developing the reasoned confidence that is constitutive of courage.

> When I wakened I was perspiring. Looking into the early
> morning sky that was growing light in the north, I went
> over it all in my mind. I saw and understood that what-
> ever I accomplished must be by my own efforts, that I
> must myself do the things I wished to do. And I knew
> that I would accomplish them if I used the powers that
> Ah-badt-dadt-deah had given me. I *had* a will and I
> would use it, make it work for me, as the Dwarf-chief
> had advised. I became very happy, lying there looking up
> into the sky. My heart began to sing like a bird, and I
> went back to the village needing no man to tell me the
> meaning of my dream. I took a sweat-bath and rested in
> my father's lodge. I *knew* myself now.[31]

Of course, Plenty Coups is recounting his childhood dream in old age—and he is telling it to a white man in order that it should be written down and preserved. Thus one should expect that there have been secondary revisions along the route from the original dream-memory when he woke up to this recounting approximately sixty-five years later. All the better! Because the Crow attributed so much importance to these dreams, there is reason to believe that the dream was recounted over and over from its childhood occurrence—and thus that the large-scale narrative structure of the dream is correct. But our project is not to uncover the original dream in all its pristine clarity; it is rather to see what role the dream might have had in the construction of Plenty Coups's character. Thus the tellings and retellings, the formations and transformations—these are what take hold in Plenty Coups's psyche. Even in old age he recounts this dream as though its meaning had been confirmed. But this persistent sense that the dream was confirmed suggests that the voice of the Dwarf-chief—one of Plenty Coups's ego-ideals—was sufficiently flexible that even in times of radical change, Plenty Coups remained confident that a courageous response was within his repertoire. Arguably this confidence contributed to his flexible-yet-courageous response to cultural collapse.

Psychoanalysts are trained to pay attention to breaks in a narrative. Linderman reports a striking moment when the chief finished his account of this dream: "Here the old Chief, as though struck with remorse, turned his head aside and whispered, 'Oh Little-people, you who have been my good Helpers through a long life, forgive me if I have done wrong in telling this to Sign-talker. I believed I was doing right. Be kind. I shall see you very soon and explain all.'"[32]

Obviously, we are not in a position to make an unimpeachable interpretation of this interlude. It was uttered in front of Linderman, so in some extended sense it might have been for his benefit. But if we just take this interlude at face value, it seems as though Plenty Coups is being interrupted in his conversation in order to respond to another call that suddenly needs tending to. The fact that he feels drawn to address the Little People suggests that they are still a live presence for him—just as he says they've been. And the fact that he appears "struck with remorse" and explicitly asks for their forgiveness suggests that the relationship has been importantly private. One way to understand this is in terms of one's relationship to the spiritual world being a private matter. This is how Plenty Coups seems to have understood it. However that may be, it is also true that a certain reticence typically characterizes one's relationship to the "spiritual world" of one's own soul. This plea for forgiveness is an indication that Plenty Coups has disclosed the wellsprings of his psyche. If the Little People— and in particular the voice of the Dwarf-chief—did function as an ego-ideal for Plenty Coups, we begin to see how he might have had the psychological ability to break through the traditional thick forms of courage and find a new, thinner form that could help the Crow through their trying times.

We began looking at Plenty Coups's prophetic dream in the previous chapter, when we were considering how one might cope with the future at a time when the standard forms of practical reason had become attenuated. The question before us now is why one might think of Plenty Coups's dream activity—and his steadfast commitment to it—not just as a means of coping, but as a human excellence. What is it about Plenty Coups's response that makes it not just a psychologically efficacious way of maintaining hope through difficult times, but a genuine manifestation of courage?

Plenty Coups had his second, prophetic dream almost a year

after his dream of the Little People. The first dream occurred when his brother had been killed and he was just nine years old; the second dream occurred when he was not yet ten. The first dream was a response to a traditional form of loss: the death of a loved one in battle against a traditional enemy. And yet, the legacy of the dream was to embed in him an authoritative voice that said he had the skills to face up to the future and flourish. We might wonder whether this first dream gave him the courage to have the second one. For in the second dream he imagines a future that is radically malign, and *still* he will have the ability to face it well and survive. It seems to me arguable that in this second dream Plenty Coups was beginning to face up to a reality that at this point—in history, in his development—he could not face in any other way. And although the dream is, of course, dreamlike, it has a disturbingly realistic tone. It is far from being purely wishful: it predicts the destruction of a way of life. It sees some powerful and malevolent forces that cannot be contained. Indeed, the dream is about facing up to destructive forces that none of the Indian tribes will be able to control. Recall that in the dream young Plenty Coups is there as the person who is experiencing the prophesy, and there is a Man-person who is a narrator and guide. In the dream, young Plenty Coups sees an old man sitting under a tree and feels pity for him. The Man-person explains to Plenty Coups that that old man is in fact Plenty Coups himself. At that very moment both the Man-person and the old man disappear.

> Instead I saw only a dark forest. A fierce storm was coming fast. The sky was black with streaks of mad color through it. I saw the Four Winds gathering to strike the

forest, and held my breath. Pity was hot in my heart for
the beautiful trees. I felt pity for all things that lived in
the forest, but was powerless to stand with them against
the Four Winds that together were making war. I
shielded my own face with my arm when they charged! I
heard the Thunders calling out in the storm, saw beautiful trees twist like blades of grass and fall in tangled piles
where the forest had been. Bending low I heard the Four
Winds rush past me as though they were not yet satis-
fied, and then I looked at the destruction they had left
behind them.

Only one tree, tall and straight, was left standing
where the great forest had stood. The Four Winds that
always make war alone had this time struck together, rid-
ing down every tree in the forest but *one*. Standing there
alone among its dead tribesmen, I thought it looked sad.
"What does this mean?" I whispered in my dream.[33]

Plenty Coups is explicitly dreaming of a historical catastrophe
of unique proportion.[34] In the past, each of the winds had made
war one at a time. Now it was to be a perfect storm. For this
dream to be a manifestation of courage—or, part of the process
by which a courageous person develops—we do not need to believe that the young dreamer is clairvoyant; only that he is imaginatively tracking, responding to, and representing reality *somehow*. The claim would be that this dream was not *just* an
imaginative fiction—a nightmare coming from his private de-
mons—but that Plenty Coups was imaginatively responding to an
impending disaster that an extraordinary young man could sense
and represent in a dream. One may question the evidentiary

value, but Plenty Coups does say to Linderman, "I was nine years old and undeveloped, but I realized the constant danger my people were in from enemies on every side."[35]

In the light of this second dream, it is useful to go back to the first dream and see that even there the winds are represented as malign, external forces over which he lacks control. In that first dream, he is taken by a person he doesn't see to a lodge filled with "Persons I did not know . . . each Person was an old warrior." When he enters there are strong voices of complaint:

> "Why have you brought this young man into our lodge?
> We do not want him. He is not our kind and therefore
> has no place among us." The words came from the south
> side, and my heart began to fall down. I looked to see
> what Persons sat on the south side, and my eyes made
> me afraid. They were the Winds, the Bad Storms, the
> Thunders, the Moon, and many Stars, all powerful, and
> each of them braver and much stronger than men . . . I
> knew that to live on the world I must concede that those
> Persons across the lodge who had not wished me to sit
> with them had work to do, and that I could not prevent
> them from doing it. I felt a little afraid but was glad I was
> there.[36]

It is in the context of these menacing, unwelcoming forces that Plenty Coups recognizes he cannot control that the Dwarf-chief welcomes him and offers him encouragement. That is, young Plenty Coups is encouraged to courage in the face of these over-whelming forces, not in ignorance of them. In Plenty Coups's imaginative life—whatever its ultimate source—these menacing external forces develop over the course of the year—from age

nine to nearly ten—into an overwhelming storm; and yet Plenty
Coups is told that he has the ability to succeed—even in the face
of this destructive reality. The world in which he has the capacity
to succeed is a world of real-life dangers and genuine risk. It is a
world in which he will succeed only if he develops and uses his
innate skills well: this is the world of the courageous person.

It is also worth considering the role of pity in the prophetic
dream. Plenty Coups says that he felt pity for all the trees
knocked down in the forest, and pity for the creatures that lived
there—though he was "powerless to stand with them against the
Four Winds." And when he looked at the old man sitting in the
shade of that lone standing tree, "I felt pity for him because he
was so old and feeble."[37] For the Crow, pity is an emotion appropriate to the gods. As we have seen, when young men went out
into nature to seek their dream-vision, they would call out to
God, "Pity me!" When they cut off a joint of a finger, made themselves bleed, starved, and became weak, they did so to invite the
pity of the spiritual world. It is from pity that the gods are moved
to help men. Thus when young Plenty Coups in the dream feels
pity, one might guess that it represents a fascinating compromise-
formation. On the one hand, Plenty Coups represents himself as
helpless in the face of inexorable sad events—hardly the kind of
wishful omnipotence one often sees in dreams. This is not a nine-
year-old boy dreaming he is superman. On the other hand, he responds with a godlike emotion. He portrays himself as able to see
these events accurately. In the dream he is viewing events *as they
shall be*, and he responds with an emotion that is appropriate to
gods and men alike. Imaginatively, we might think of extraordinary men as inhabiting a space between gods and ordinary men.
The true heroes are intermediate figures—mortals who can com-

municate with the divine. But if we think of the psychological process by which courage develops in an individual soul, young Plenty Coups is imaginatively giving himself the resources to experience reality as the gods would. Part of what it is to be courageous is to see reality accurately and to respond well in the face of it. Plenty Coups is envisaging a scene that is genuinely pitiable— the gods would see it that way—and yet, even in these circumstances, he is able to respond and act well. The point is not that he is dreaming that he can do this; it is that his dreaming equips him with the psychological resources actually to be able to do it.

Courage, Aristotle tells us, requires the ability to face up to reality, to exercise good judgment, and to tolerate danger in doing so. One way to explore the depth of a person's courage is to inquire into the range of experience in which a person can do just that. What kind of constancy can a person maintain across life's experiences? A traditional courageous warrior would be able to face anything that might arise in battle. Thus we apprehend the truly courageous warrior in terms of the extremes of battle experience. A person demonstrates his ability to act courageously over a range of experience when he can continue to act well at its limits. As would be expected, Crow tales of courage are of extraordinary deeds—for this is the realm in which true courage comes to light.[38] But, as we have seen, the truly courageous warrior who could face anything in battle might be utterly unequipped to face a reality in which battle becomes irrelevant. His training in youth may have equipped him to face all foreseeable possibilities; but what has emerged in his time are new types of possibility. There are now new limits opening up to the possibilities of experience. How is one to face the reality that a way of facing reality is coming to an end? It looks as though Plenty Coups's dream life is giving him just the kind of psychological resources he needs to face this new reality well.

One of the salutary effects of his dream is to inoculate him against the problem of evil. The Crow believe that they are a chosen people: chosen by God to flourish on this particular land. The problem of evil arises when a religious people are faced with horrific historical circumstances. They ask, "How could a good and powerful God allow this to happen to us?" The problem is especially pressing when God seems to remain silent. When Plenty Coups had his dream, the Crow were about to face the worst century in their history. There were to be punishing battles with the Sioux, confinement to the reservation, terrible disease and mortality at Crow Agency. But Plenty Coups's dream anticipates that a terrible storm is coming; so when these bad events occur, they are seen as *confirming* the dream. The dream is taken as coming from a spiritual source, and it gives an explanation of the disaster. The Four Winds are natural-spiritual forces that have overwhelming power, but their menacing existence does not disturb the very fabric of the universe. The world is a place in which such a storm can occur. It is possible for humans to be overwhelmed in this way, but the fundamental goodness of the world is secure. Also, the dream, as interpreted, gives divine sanction for the thought that *if* the Crow can use their wisdom—the wisdom of the chickadee—they can survive. Plenty Coups adopts this interpretation and remains steadfast in his commitment to it. Thus the message of the dream, while pessimistic, also holds out hope. And it leaves intact the idea that the Crow have a special place. Plenty Coups's dream is interpreted by the elders as saying that the original divine promise will be sustained: if they follow the wisdom of the chickadee, they will survive and hold onto their land. Even today, if one visits the museum in Plenty Coups State Park in Pryor, Montana, one will see this plaque:

> Our elders interpreted his vision to mean that the white people would take over Indian country, and that the Chickadee's lodge represented the Crow tribe, which placed its lodge in the right place. Today we retain the heart of Crow country as our reservation.

In this way, the dream provides the psychological resources by which one might avoid despair. But for this hope to count as a constituent of courage, rather than as a mere wishful optimism, we must see it as facilitating the capacity to respond well to reality. For Plenty Coups and the Crow, the dream had a divine sanction; and this belief played a significant role in their ability to hold onto its significance. We can remain agnostic about that claim and nevertheless argue that the dream manifested courage—and contributed to its development. All we need to maintain is that the dream was itself a creative response to reality and that as a response it was not entirely wishful but actually provided good advice. The prediction in the interpreted dream is not that things will work out for the Crow no matter what, but that after an inevitable devastation, the Crow will survive and hold onto their land *if* they make the best use of their own skills to learn from others. The historical record gives credence to the idea that this was good advice. It is, I think, arguable that the Crow ended up better off by following this advice than they would have by any other strategy. And, in particular, despair would have made them worse off in terms of dealing with life's challenges. In this way it is arguable that the hope embedded in Plenty Coups's dream was an important constituent of courage. The aim is not to make an a priori argument that such a strategy will always be courageous. We must rely on our own best judgment—and our best judgment of what counts as the best judgment of others—to make up our minds about what counts as genuine courage. But if we examine the details of these decisions and acts, a plausible case can be made that they were a manifestation of courage.

## Historical Vindication

The Crow were not able magically to turn the tide of history. The onslaught of the white man was a force that no Indian tribe could resist. That outcome is just as the dream predicted. The question is whether the hopefulness manifest in the dream facilitated a courageous response to the new challenges the Crow would face. To the extent that the dream was confirmed—that the Crow did survive and did hold onto their land—what role did that hope play in securing this outcome? I think it can be shown that the role was considerable.

On the basis of Plenty Coups's dream, the tribe decided to ally with the United States against its traditional enemies. They participated in common battles against the Sioux and celebrated the defeats that were inflicted upon them.[39] And the U.S. government did treat the Crow as an ally. This fact did not stop the United States from repeatedly revising treaties at will and from encroaching on Crow lands. But, unlike other tribes, the Crow were not displaced from their lands, they were not put on a forced march, they did not have to walk a "trail of tears"—and they could correctly say of themselves that they were never defeated.[40]

Their undefeated status remains a source of pride among the Crow. Plenty Coups was received at the highest levels of the U.S. government in Washington—as were other Crow chiefs—and treated with respect. And although they suffered many strategic setbacks, the Crow were able to leverage for themselves a better outcome than they could have done by pursuing any other strategy. In this way the dream helped them to face up to this new reality and to deal with it in imaginative, resourceful, yet steadfast ways.

A paradigm is the sequence of negotiations that led to the Crow Act of 1920. Although the Crow had retained some of their land, the United States put pressure on them to divide it up, allotting individual properties to the members of the tribe. Such a change posed a threat to the survival of the tribal lands, as Plenty Coups well recognized: once the lands were allotted, the individual farms might later be sold—and the Crow reservation could be broken up piece by piece. This threat followed an even greater one in 1915, when the U.S. senators from Montana proposed that all the unallotted land west of the Big Horn and east of Little Big Horn be opened to homesteaders; individual Crows who already had their own allotted farms would be able to keep them. This measure, if passed, would have appropriated all the land that the Crow tribe still held communally.[41] In January 1917, Plenty Coups led a delegation to Washington that lobbied successfully to prevent the bill from coming to the Senate floor. After World War I, in 1919, the issue arose again. The Senate Indian Affairs Committee told the tribe that no bill would pass without their approval *provided* the Crow ended the practice of communally held land. This proposition sparked a debate within the tribe. Plenty Coups argued for resisting any further changes; some of the younger leaders, like Robert Yellowtail, a lawyer educated in the white man's school, saw allotment as a way to avoid further white encroachment. The younger leaders won the day, and the Crow Act became law in 1920.

This sequence of events is an example of what Aristotle would call a mixed action.[42] The Crow had to act in difficult circumstances. Plenty Coups was not able to avoid the allotment of reservation lands. But the tribe was able to negotiate significant successes. The tribe retained all mineral rights to the land under its control. Although the land was allotted, it was retained by members of the tribe. It defeated the attempt to sell off "unused" land to white settlers. And, perhaps most important, the tribe was able to set the conditions under which the allotment took place. Further, the legislation set a precedent that endured: no further large-scale land offerings would be approved by Congress. Given the previous seventy years of encroachments, of treaty revisions and land-grabs, the outcome represents a significant success.

And though Plenty Coups lost that last debate within the tribe, the nature of that defeat actually confirmed the ideals that were given to him in the dream. The chickadee survives because he is able to learn from others. Thus Plenty Coups had urged the young men and women of the tribe to be educated in the white man's schools. Even today he is remembered for telling his people: "With what the white man knows he can oppress us. If we learn what he knows, he can never oppress us again."[43] Robert Yellowtail had followed this advice. And it was precisely from his study of U.S. law and American politics that he came to think that fashioning a distinctively Crow approach to allotment would ultimately be the best way to protect Crow lands. Arguably, this is the wisdom of the chickadee unto the second generation. The tribe survived and protected its interests by following the ideals that Plenty Coups advocated, even when the specific decision went against his own judgment.

Even in old age, Plenty Coups was able to wrest certain individual successes. Just a few months before his death in 1932, he asked tribal attorneys to petition the U.S. government to protect the Pryor and Big Horn Mountains from allotment—and he succeeded. These mountains remain protected. He also succeeded in having the trust period for allotments extended by twenty-six years. The result was that although individual Crow would have allotments, they would not receive title to the land—and thus not be able to sell it—until that extended period was up.[44] Today members of the tribe express pride that the Crow were able to keep their mountains; and there is at least discussion of how the tribe might over time be able to buy back lands that members have sold to white farmers. There is also discussion about how the tribe might discourage future such sales.

There is another historical accomplishment that is harder to measure. Plenty Coups laid down an enduring collective ideal for the tribe as it faced new challenges. He drew upon ancient tribal beliefs—the chickadee has long been respected among the Crow—and put them to new use. He insisted that his people learn the white man's ways, but he idealized neither the white man nor his own tribe. The white man, he said, "too often promised to do one thing and then, when [he] acted at all, did another." He is someone "who fools nobody but himself."[45] "With all his wonderful powers, the white man is not wise. He is smart, but not wise."[46] He was no easier on his tribe. At feasts, he would lecture them: "You who once were brave have turned into pigs. I am ashamed of you. Self-pity has stolen your courage, robbed you of your spirit and self-respect. Stop mourning the old days, they are gone with the buffalo. Go to your sweatlodges and cleanse your bodies . . . then clean out your dirty lodges and go to work!"[47] Yet he hoped that a new generation would be able to hold onto traditional Crow values and customs while synthesizing them with a white man's education.

In the historical circumstances, this seems a hopeful-yet-realistic response. For in addition to all the objective degradations the various Indian tribes had to endure, they had to suffer an assault on their subjectivity. At the end of the nineteenth and beginning of the twentieth centuries, it was official U.S. policy to break down traditional tribal values. Accordingly, certain traditional rituals and religious practices were forbidden by law; children were forcibly separated from their parents and put in the white man's schools; and, as we have seen, there was relentless pressure to break up tribal lands and turn the members of the tribe into individual farmers. In any case, the traditional way of life was destroyed. So it is hard to see how, in these circumstances, any ideals could survive. A crucial aspect of psychological health depends on the internalization of vibrant ideals—the formation of a culturally enriched ego-ideal—in relation to which one can strive to live a rewarding life. Without such ideals, it is difficult to see what there is to live for. Many factors contribute to the alcoholism and drug abuse that plague the Indian reservations; no doubt, unemployment and poverty play crucial roles. But there is also the psychological devastation for young teenagers when they cannot find ideals worthy of internalizing and making their own.

For a vibrant culture, it is traditionally the task of the older generation to adapt the culture's ideals to current challenges and to pass those ideals on to the next generation. But in the period 1870–1940, the Crow tribe went through such a collective disruption that there was no way to pass on those ideals in an unproblematic way. It was in this context that Plenty Coups drew on traditional tribal resources—the chickadee—to formulate an *ego-ideal of radical hope*. That is, he gave the tribe the possibility of drawing on a traditional ideal that would help them endure a loss of concepts. I am tempted to say that during their nomadic-warrior period no Crow could have dreamed of the uses to which the traditional icon of the chickadee would eventually be put. Except that one of them did. Even he could not dream in detail about the chickadee's future. But this ideal gave the Crow a basis of hope at a time when it was systematically unclear what one could hope for. Plenty Coups's dream held out for the Crow the hope that if they followed the wisdom of the chickadee (whatever that would come to mean) they would survive (whatever that would come to mean) and hold onto their lands (whatever that would come to mean). Thus Plenty Coups bequeathed an ideal that would help the tribe tolerate a period of conceptual devastation. And the fact that this ideal has survived—that is, that a traditional ideal has a vibrant life on the other side of this abyss—lends legitimacy to the claim that the Crow have indeed survived. Or, perhaps, that the Crow have *revived*.

That Plenty Coups could formulate such an ideal and pass it along—at a time when traditional ideals were losing their vibrancy—is, I think, his greatest achievement. Plenty Coups's ideal remains a powerful legacy. His exhortation to education is the credo of Little Big Horn College, which educates students on the reservation in Crow history and tradition, but also in algebra, accounting, economics, computing, psychology, and the humanities. It is a living monument to his ideal. I have had the privi-

lege of talking to young members of the Crow Nation—students
on the reservation and at Little Big Horn National Monument,
as well as students and interns in Washington, D.C., and Chicago—and I have repeatedly been told that in childhood Plenty
Coups's words were drilled into them. In their articulateness, vibrancy, knowledge of events, and plans for the future—and in
their ability to interact comfortably with whites and Indians—one
will, I think, see the living legacy of Plenty Coups's hope. This
was not merely wishful optimism but a sustained thoughtful en-
gagement with the world that, in terrible circumstances, yielded
tangible positive results.

### Personal Vindication

Plenty Coups felt vindicated by his life choices. As he told
Linderman:

> The Crow were wiser [than the Sioux and Cheyenne].
> We knew the white men were strong, without number in
> their own country, and that there was no good in fighting
> them . . . Our leading chiefs saw that to help the white
> men fight their enemies and ours would make them our
> friends. We had always fought the three tribes, Sioux,
> Cheyenne and Arapahoe, anyway, and might as well do
> so now. The complete destruction of our old enemies
> would please us. Our decision was reached, not because
> we loved the white man who was already crowding other
> tribes into our country, or because we hated the Sioux,

Cheyenne and Arapahoe, but because we plainly saw
that this course was the only one which might save our
beautiful country for us. When I think back my heart
sings because we acted as we did. It was the only way
open to us.[48]

Look at our country! It was chosen by my people out of
the heart of the most beautiful land on all the world, because we were wise. And it was my dream that taught us
the way.[49]

In old age Plenty Coups could see that the Crow had been able
to hold onto their lands. As history unfolded, the very idea of what
it was to hold onto one's land changed radically, but the elderly
Plenty Coups could nevertheless see his boyhood dream as having been confirmed by experience. Indeed, as he was recounting his tale to Linderman—as he was telling him that prophetic
dream—he was sitting on the very spot where the dream had
placed him. "And here I am, an old man, sitting under this tree
just where that old man sat seventy years ago when this was a different world."[50] He had brought himself to the spot where the
dream told him he would be. And the recitation of the dream to
Linderman was in its own way the triumphal counting of coup:
he was telling the story of how he successfully went to "battle" to
protect his land. He was now sitting under the tree that the dream
told him he would if he adopted the virtue of the chickadee.

At Plenty Coups's home, that tree is still standing. And his
house is now a state park. Plenty Coups got the idea of donating
his house when he visited Mt. Vernon, George Washington's
house. Here is an instance of taking up a white man's idea in order to establish an institution that would preserve and transmit

traditional Crow values. Plenty Coups and his wife Strikes the Iron wanted to will his house and property to the U.S. government to be "set apart as a park and recreation ground for the members of the Crow Tribe of Indians and white people jointly . . . in trust and perpetuity." In one of history's ironies, the U.S. government took itself to be unable to accept the land *as a gift!* It seems that the government could only take land, not accept it. And, adding insult to injury, government agents decided to mislead and patronize Plenty Coups: "It was the intention of Plenty Coups to will his property to the United States Government. It was found that this could not be done, but the government went through the motions of accepting the farm so as not to offend the kindly old chief. An elaborate ceremony took place at his home on August 8, 1928."[51] When he died the county commissioners took charge of the property; and finally the Billings Kiwanis Club trustees were able to take charge of the land and restore the property.[52] Eventually influential members arranged to donate it to the State of Montana—and it now functions as a park, as Plenty Coups wanted. And so, Plenty Coups not only saw his dream as confirmed; he had reason to think that his steadfast commitment to his dream played a crucial role in his successfully negotiating a future for his tribe. Though they faced a terrible onslaught upon their civilization, they did hold onto their precious land, and they did hold onto the possibility of transmitting their values and memories of their traditions to another generation. Indeed, telling Linderman his story was arguably the last act of Plenty Coups the chickadee. For part of the white man's wisdom was literacy: the value of writing memories down is that it can preserve them through times when an oral culture may be under too much stress to hold onto them. The chickadee understands that in a period of cultural onslaught one not only needs an ideal like the chickadee; one also needs to learn new ways to preserve and transmit it. That is what Plenty Coups was doing—and his ideals and memories are there today for a new generation of Crow to pick up and transform for themselves.

Thus I think the case is made not just that it was psychologically advantageous not to give in to despair but also that it would have been a mistake to do so. It would also have been a mistake to "go down fighting." The radical hope that was embedded in the ideal of the chickadee helped Plenty Coups throughout his life to make creative decisions in radically new historical circumstances. And his fidelity to hope fits all of Aristotle's hallmarks of courage. With the virtue of the chickadee he was able to reorient himself to what was genuinely shameful (criterion 1)—and to teach others. What would be shameful now would be to turn one's back on the *genuine* wisdom of others; to give in to despair; to nostalgically insist that one can go back to the old ways without any change. At a certain historical point, feeling ashamed that you can no longer live as a traditional warrior may be psychologically understandable, but it is a mistake. By providing an ideal for the times, Plenty Coups did not merely give himself and his people the psychological resources to adapt to a new situation; he also gave them an ideal in relation to which they could aim for something fine (criterion 2). The aim was not merely the biological survival of the individual members of the tribe—however important that was—but the future flourishing of traditional tribal values, customs, and memories in a new context. This is an admirable goal. Moreover, the virtue of the chickadee explicitly advocates developing good judgment, and making decisions on how to act that are based on knowledge (criterion 3). This has been ev-

ident in the tribe's defense of its land. And Plenty Coups's strategy
has involved serious risk (criterion 4). This was not the paradigm
risk of death on the battlefield, to be sure. It was a greater risk:
that one had reoriented oneself toward shame in the wrong sort of
way, and was unwittingly doing something shameful, not fine;
that one's strategy would not ultimately work and that the Crow
would lose their land, their values—indeed, that they would be
destroyed as a people. The stakes could not have been higher for
Plenty Coups and his people. Finally, it has been the aim of this
entire chapter to argue that Plenty Coups's radical hope was not
mere wish-fulfilling optimism (criterion 5), but was rather a radical form of hope that constituted courage and made it possible.
After all, through a series of canny decisions and acts, the Crow
were able to hold onto their land, and Plenty Coups helped to
create a space in which traditional Crow values can be preserved
in memory, transmitted to a new generation, and, one hopes, re-
newed in a new historical era.

This was possible because Plenty Coups was able to bring
about an astonishing imaginative transformation. Through his
dream—and his fidelity to it—Plenty Coups was able to transform the destruction of a *telos* into a teleological suspension of
the ethical. A traditional way of life was being destroyed, and
along with it came the destruction of its conception of the good
life. The nature of human happiness became essentially unclear
and problematic. In such conditions, the temptation to despair is
all but overwhelming. And it was in just such a moment that
Plenty Coups's dream predicted that destruction and offered an
image of salvation—and a route to it. The traditional forms of living a good life were going to be destroyed, but there was spiritual
backing for the thought that new good forms of living would arise

for the Crow, if only they would adhere to the virtues of the chickadee.

It is worth noting the role played by enigma in making this imaginative transformation possible. For starters, Plenty Coups's name is not, strictly speaking, Plenty Coups, but rather "Many Achievements" (Alaxchiiahush). Certainly, his grandfather, who named him, envisaged that he would count many coups. Nevertheless, his name is strictly Many Achievements—and what constitutes an achievement is open for re-interpretation in the light of experience. This name functions as what psychoanalysts call an *enigmatic signifier*: it is given to him by a parental figure, and thus it has for him a kind of oracular status. It tells him who he is or will be while remaining enigmatic in meaning.[53] This is what can get lost in the shift to "Plenty Coups": Many Achievements—Alaxchiiahush—knows he will achieve great things, but the nature of the achievements is left vague. Ironically, one of his important achievements involved *abandoning* coup. So, too, the virtue of the chickadee is essentially enigmatic. The chickadee has the ability to learn from the wisdom of others—but it is left systematically unclear what this wisdom is. That is for the chickadee to find out.

The fixed point in this enigmatic story is the interpretation the elders gave to young Plenty Coups's dream: that if the man of many achievements follows the wisdom of the chickadee, the Crow will be able to retain their land. This interpretation adds symbolic poignancy to the image of old Plenty Coups, sitting under the tree of the chickadee, recounting his story to Linderman. The planting of a coup-stick in battle was symbolic of a tree that cannot be felled. Yet there Plenty Coups is, at the end of his life, sitting under an actual tree that history has proved cannot be felled. In giving up the symbol of protecting Crow territory he actually succeeded in protecting it. He used the dream to reach down to the imaginative strategies that might save Crow land; and in so doing he substituted the symbol of the tree that cannot be felled for the tree that cannot be felled. An actual tree became its own symbol. It is still there, marking a real boundary of Crow territory.

Plenty Coups's dream—and his fidelity to it—also enabled him to live what Aristotle would call a complete life. In spite of the devastation to traditional Crow life, Plenty Coups's dream became a thread through which he could lead his people through radical discontinuity. In sticking to his dream, he unified his life across this discontinuity: and at the end of his biological life, he was able to see his life as having a unity and a purpose that was confirmed by the unfolding of events. Indeed, *the repetition of his story to Linderman is its completion.* In telling his story, he presented himself as having had a complete life; and he was able to pass on to a future generation what he thought was still essential to the Crow way of life.

### Response to Sitting Bull

Sitting Bull in his visit to the Crow reservation was harshly critical of the ideals Plenty Coups taught. Only a fool would cooperate with the white man, he argued, and no authentic leader of the Crow would lead them in this direction. Both these leaders command our respect; and our aim is not to sit in judgment of either of them. Rather, we are inquiring into the legitimate roles that hope and imagination might play in the formation and development of courageous ways of living. Still, Sitting Bull has laid down a challenge; and it behooves us to consider what response might be made on Plenty Coups's behalf. In this section, I am going to be a straightforward advocate for Plenty Coups's vision in opposition to Sitting Bull's.

In 1889 there was much talk throughout the Sioux reservation of the coming of a new messiah who would save the Indians. In the fall, a delegation of tribal leaders rode west, from where the rumors were coming, and in the winter they wrote back confirming the news.[54] When they returned in the spring of 1890 they said there was a person who said he was the son of God, who had once been killed by whites, who bore the scars of crucifixion, and who claimed that he had returned to punish the whites and restore the Indians to their previous life. This seems to have been the famous Wovoka, a holy man who is generally credited with having introduced the peyote religion to the Indian tribes of the South and West. According to this messiah, in the following spring (1891), he would wipe out all whites in a catastrophe, bring back their ancestors from the dead, restore all the buffalo. These emissaries reported that they had even seen a number of dead relatives who were alive, as well as a herd of buffalo.[55]

The messiah was teaching that the current task of the Indian was to perform a Ghost Dance, which would help usher in the apocalypse. The dance spread like wildfire across the reservation, but nowhere did it take greater hold than at Sitting Bull's camp at Standing Rock. The dance was ecstatic: participants would dance into a frenzy and continue until they dropped of exhaustion; they wore ghost shirts that would protect them from bullets; they abandoned all other activities in order to bring about this cataclysm.

There is no evidence that Sitting Bull actually participated in the Ghost Dance, but he did support it. The dance began at Standing Rock on October 9, inaugurated at Sitting Bull's invitation. And when officers came to arrest Kicking Bear, who was introducing the dance, Sitting Bull promised that Kicking Bear would go back to his reservation, but the Ghost Dance would continue. They had received a message from the spirit world that they must do so.[56] The dance continued through October and November and into December, when it was forcibly ended. As is well documented, U.S. authorities were greatly disturbed by the Ghost Dance—they were concerned it might lead to an uprising or, at least, the breakdown of civil order—and they sought to suppress it. On December 15, 1890, as tribal police tried to arrest Sitting Bull on orders of the Indian agent, he was killed by police in the midst of an outbreak of violence.

His death is a national disgrace. And while much deserves to be said about Sitting Bull's right to religious expression as well as the ineptitude and brutality of the response, still, from Plenty Coups's perspective, Sitting Bull deployed religious imagination in the wrong sort of way. The point here is not whether one was for or against working with the white man or learning from him. Rather, it is that Sitting Bull used a dream-vision to short-circuit reality rather than to engage with it. We do not have to adjudicate whether this dream-vision was or was not coming from a spiritual source. From Plenty Coups's perspective, even if the dream did come from the spirit world, it was being misinterpreted and misapplied: Sitting Bull deployed a messianic vision that fueled the Ghost Dance in a wishful way. It is a hallmark of the wishful that the world will be magically transformed—into conformity with how one would like it to be—without having to take any realistic practical steps to bring it about. The only activity in which one is enjoined to partake is a ritual, in this case a dance. But when the ritual comes to take over one's entire life, as it did for the Sioux at Standing Rock in the fall of 1890, this is a case of what Freud called "turning away from reality." Symbolic rituals take over life—whether in an individual's private life or in the group activity of a culture—and they become a way of avoiding the real-life demands that confront one in the everyday. And it led to a disaster for the Sioux.

In a sense, Plenty Coups and Sitting Bull had the same vision, but they interpreted it in opposite ways. Both saw the ghosts of buffalo, but for Plenty Coups the vision signified they were going away forever; for Sitting Bull and his Sioux followers, it signified that they were coming back.[57] This is a danger for all forms of messianic religions: a wish can easily be mistaken for reality. In the case of the Ghost Dance, the outcome is strong evidence that Sitting Bull's people used it in a wish-fulfilling way.

Plenty Coups was outspoken in his opposition to the messianic peyote religion that was sweeping across the Indian tribes.[58] And his opposition brings to light a significant philosophical issue: there will always be a question, and thus a possibility for debate, around what counts as traditional. Sitting Bull was trying to preserve the traditional Sioux way of life. But to that end, he adopted a ritual that was entirely new—and that had itself arisen in response to painful defeat. The Native American Church, which evolved out of the messianic peyote religion, sees itself as preserving traditional Indian culture—and no doubt it does in various ways; but it is also true that the idea of a pan-Indian church would have been alien to the tribes before they encountered white culture. I have heard young members of the Crow tribe express skepticism about the pan-Indian movement. They take it as a symptom of the defeat that was inflicted on the other tribes. The Crow, in their opinion, were able to retain their distinctively Crow rituals. And thus, for them, pan-Indian rituals are ways of watering down their uniquely Crow heritage.

As we saw in the first chapter, the Crow actually stopped performing their Sun Dance in 1875; and when it was re-introduced in 1941, they had to learn the steps of the Shoshone version.[59] The dance is now organized around heartfelt requests—for example, that a young girl survive a heart operation. Is this the maintenance or re-introduction of a tradition—or is the name of "tradition" being invoked to invent new rituals? It is not for me to answer this question: that is and will be the task of Crow poets, of Crow leaders and their followers. But I can say that Plenty Coups has bequeathed them the wherewithal to reinvigorate a genuine tradition. In this context, Plenty Coups's haunting statement, "After this, nothing happened," takes on a new meaning. Plenty Coups had to acknowledge the destruction of a *telos*—that the old ways of living a good life were gone. And that acknowledgment involved the stark recognition that the traditional ways of structuring significance—of recognizing something as a happening—had been devastated. For Plenty Coups, this recognition was not an expression of despair; it was the only way to avoid it. One needs to recognize the destruction that has occurred if one is to move beyond it. In the abstract, there is no answer to the question: Is the Sun Dance the maintenance of a sacred tradition or is it a nostalgic evasion—a step or two away from a Disneyland imitation of "the Indian"? What is valuable about Plenty Coups's declaration is that it lays down a crucial fact that needs to be acknowledged if a genuinely vibrant tradition is to be maintained or reintroduced. It is one thing to dance as though nothing has happened; it is another to acknowledge that something singularly awful has happened—the collapse of happenings—and then decide to dance.

Plenty Coups was also able to preserve some of the traditional warrior ideals in this radically new context. As we saw in the first chapter, at the dedication ceremony of the Tomb of the Unknown Soldier Plenty Coups laid down his coup-stick and his headdress. But he also declared a new role for the Crow warrior:

> For the Indians of America I call upon the Great Spirit
> of the Red men with gesture and tribal tongue: That the
> dead should not have died in vain; That war might end;
> That peace be purchased by the blood of Red Men and
> White.[60]

If one visits the Veterans' Memorial at the Crow Agency today one will see a list of distinguished Crow veterans who have served with or in the U.S. military from the original Sioux wars, through World Wars I and II, the Korean War, Vietnam, Panama, Afghanistan, and Iraq. On the wall there is a plaque, "Warrior's Homecoming," which begins:

> The Crow Tribe . . . practices its own style and brand of
> ceremonies and rituals. These are practices that have
> been with The Tribe for generations and centuries. One
> which has regained attention recently is a ceremony to
> welcome returning combat veterans. This is done today
> as before by The Tribe since early times when The Crow
> were largely a Warrior Society. It is called Warrior's

Homecoming (literally translated as "bring-back-to-the-camp-home/tribe").[61]

There follows a description of how to perform the ceremony as well as advice about how to think about its meaning in these new historical circumstances. Thus a direct link is made between the ancient warrior values and the new and available role of combat veteran.[62] And Plenty Coups's words paved the way.

Finally, as we have seen in detail, Plenty Coups was able to draw upon the traditional icon of the chickadee. Through his dream-vision, Plenty Coup was able to take a valued and honored spiritual force and put it to creative use in facing up to new challenges. Thus, although Plenty Coups was advocating a new way of life for the Crow, he was drawing upon the past in vibrant ways. And thus I think a case can be made that Plenty Coups offered the Crow a *traditional* way of going forward.

Notes

Acknowledgments

Index

# Notes

## I. After This, Nothing Happened

1. Frank B. Linderman, *Plenty-Coups: Chief of the Crows* (Lincoln: University of Nebraska Press, 1962), pp. 308–309. The book was originally published under the title *American: The Life Story of a Great Indian*. There is also a new edition—*Plenty-Coups, Chief of the Crows* (Lincoln: University of Nebraska Press, 2002)—which contains a new essay by the author about meeting Plenty Coups, an insightful "Afterword" on Plenty Coups's place in recent Crow history by Timothy McCleary, and an introduction by Barney Old Coyote Jr. and Phenocia Bauerle. A note on usage: throughout this book I use the terms "white man" and "Indian." Although some may experience these terms as offensive, (1) they are the terms in which Plenty Coups understood his situation; and (2) the members of the Crow tribe whom I know prefer to call themselves Indians rather than Native Americans, Native Peoples, etc., and they inform me that the term is a shared preference among the Crow.

2. Linderman, *Plenty-Coups*, p. vii.

3. Ibid., p. 311.

4. This principle is also known as the "principle of charity," and the most famous arguments for it are given by Donald Davidson. See his "Radical Interpretation," in *Inquiries into Truth and Interpretation* (Oxford: Clarendon Press, 1984), pp. 136–137; "Belief and the Basis of Meaning," ibid., pp. 152–153; "Thought and Talk," ibid.,

pp. 168–169; "On the Very Idea of a Conceptual Scheme," ibid., pp. 196–197; "The Method of Truth in Metaphysics," ibid., pp. 200–201.

5. See Frederick E. Hoxie, *Parading through History: The Making of the Crow Nation in America, 1805–1935* (Cambridge: Cambridge University Press, 1997), pp. 259–261. This marvelous book is a sine qua non for anyone interested in Crow history. See also Mardell Hogan Plainfeather, "Plenty Coups (Alaxchiiaahush)," in *Encyclopedia of North American Indians* (Houghton Mifflin: online).

6. He may even be our tax collector: see Johannes de Silentio (Søren Kierkegaard), *Fear and Trembling: Dialectical Lyric*, ed. and trans. H. V. Hong and E. H. Hong (Princeton: Princeton University Press, 1983), pp. 38–41.

7. Marshall Sahlins, *Islands of History* (Chicago: University of Chicago Press, 1985), p. xiv. What Sahlins actually says in the text needs one emendation. He says: "an event is not simply a phenomenal happening, even though as a phenomenon it has reasons and forces of its own, apart from any given symbolic scheme. An event becomes such as it is interpreted." And he continues: "The event is a *relation* between a happening and a structure (or structures): an encompassment of the phenomenon-in-itself as a meaningful value, from which follows its historical efficacy." Sahlins seems to take a "phenomenal happening" to be a kind of extratheoretical something that in conjunction with a cultural scheme gives us an event. His assumption that "phenomenal happenings" are given is problematic, but we can see the general point Sahlins is making: neither events nor happenings are isolated atoms that exist independently of a theoretical framework or "cultural scheme." It is rather these frameworks that locate "happenings" in an explanatory and meaning-filled context. This insight is as true of physics as it is of local cultures. If we think of space and time as fixed structures, which are capable of being represented on a gridlike map, then it makes sense to ask what is happening at a given point in space at a given moment in time. That framework gives us a basis for think-

ing we have a concept of a physical event. If we should lose this conception of space and time—if, for instance, it should become puzzling what counts as a point in space or a moment in time—then it again becomes puzzling what should count as a physical event. See also Roy Wagner, *The Invention of Culture* (Chicago: University of Chicago Press, 1981).

8. Sahlins, *Islands of History*, p. vii.

9. Joseph Medicine Crow, *From the Heart of Crow Country* (1992; reprint, Lincoln: University of Nebraska Press, 2000), p. 21. This fascinating book gives the Crow perspective on their history.

10. Ibid., p. 2. And see Frederick Hoxie, *The Crow* (New York: Chelsea House, 1989), p. 29.

11. Robert H. Lowie, *The Crow Indians* (Lincoln: University of Nebraska Press, 1983), p. 215. For a fascinating account of the significance of the Tobacco Society, see Peter Nabokov, "Cultivating Themselves: The Interplay of Crow Indian Religion and History" (Ph.D. diss., University of California, Berkeley, 1988).

12. Lowie, *The Crow Indians*, p. 218.

13. The word "coup" (blow) comes from the French word—the influence of French trappers and traders—and it entered the Indian-English argot of the frontier. The Crow words for "coup" are *alaxch-iia* and *da\*akshe*; for "coup-stick," *baláxxiihachke* and *kakeé*. See Ishtaléesgua Báachiia Héeleetaalawe (Squirrel That Walks among the Pines) and Mary Helen Medicine Horse, comps., *A Dictionary of Everyday Crow* (Crow Agency, Minn.: Bilingual Materials Development Center, 1987) p. 122.

14. Linderman, *Plenty-Coups*, p. 54; Lowie, *The Crow Indians*, p. 184.

15. Lowie, *The Crow Indians*, pp. 183–196.

16. Ibid., p. 331. For a traditional Crow story of such a person, see "Rabbit Child: A Crazy Dog of the Crows," in *The Way of the Warrior: Stories of the Crow People*, ed. Phenocia Bauerle, comp. and trans. Henry Old Coyote and Barney Old Coyote Jr. (Lincoln: University of Nebraska Press, 2003), pp. 27–38.

17. Lowie, *The Crow Indians*, p. 184.

18. Linderman, *Plenty-Coups*, pp. 55–56. See also Lowie, *The Crow Indians*, pp. 184–195; Joseph Medicine Crow, *From the Heart of Crow Country*, p. 45; and Glendolin Damon Wagner and Dr. William A. Allen, *Blankets and Moccasins: Plenty Coups and His People, the Crows* (1933; reprint, Lincoln: University of Nebraska Press, 1987), p. 162; Rodney Frey, *The World of the Crow Indians: As Driftwood Lodges* (Norman: University of Oklahoma Press, 1987), pp. 21–22; Frank B. Linderman, *Pretty-Shield: Medicine Woman of the Crows* (Lincoln: University of Nebraska Press, 1974), p. 44; Clara Ehrlich, "Tribal Culture in Crow Mythology," *Journal of American Folk-Lore* 50 (1937), 307–408; see especially 348–350.

19. Aristotle, *Nicomachean Ethics* 3.6–9, in *Aristotelis Ethica Nicomachea*, ed. I. Bywater (Oxford: Oxford University Press, 1980). Two especially good English translations are *Nicomachean Ethics*, ed. S. Broadie, trans. C. Rowe (Oxford: Oxford University Press, 2000); and *Nicomachean Ethics*, in *The Complete Works of Aristotle*, ed. J. Barnes, 2 vols. (Princeton: Princeton University Press, 1984), 2: 1729–1867.

20. Lowie, *The Crow Indians*, p. 228.

21. Linderman, *Plenty-Coups*, pp. 27–28; Plainfeather, "Plenty Coups (Alaxchiiaahush)." I discuss the significance of Plenty Coups's name in the final chapter.

22. This incident was recorded by Dr. William Allen, who at various times was a hunter, goldseeker, blacksmith, and dentist, but who formed a friendship with Plenty Coups that stretched over decades. See Wagner and Allen, *Blankets and Moccasins*, p. 118.

23. Lowie, *The Crow Indians*, pp. 228–229. Even Linderman is puzzled by the act, for he notes: "if a warrior was wounded in counting coup, the feather he wore to mark the event must be painted red to show that he bled. Strangely enough from our point of view, this was not considered so great an honor as escaping unharmed"; *Plenty-Coups*, p. 56.

24. Richard White, "The Winning of the West: The Expansion of the Western Sioux in the Eighteenth and Nineteenth Centuries," *Jour-*

one by D. F. Swenson and W. Lowrie (Princeton: Princeton University Press, 1941); and one by H. V. Hong and E. H. Hong (Princeton: Princeton University Press, 1992). I discuss this conception of subjectivity in detail in *Therapeutic Action: An Earnest Plea for Irony* (New York: Other Press, 2003), pp. 29–88.

51. Online: http://lib.lbhc.cc.mt.us/old_site_backup/plentyco.htm.

52. Linderman, *Pretty-Shield*, p. 8.

53. I discuss the earnestness of this type of irony in "Socratic Method and Psychoanalysis," in *The Blackwell Companion to Socrates*, ed. S. Rappe (London: Blackwell, 2005); and in *Therapeutic Action*.

54. I am indebted to John Haugeland's phenomenology of the game of chess. See "Objective Perception" and "Truth and Rule Following," in Haugeland, *Having Thought* (Cambridge, Mass.: Harvard University Press, 2000), pp. 241–265, 305–361. See also Aristotle's comment that a human being without a polis is like an isolated checkers piece; Aristotle, *Politics* 1.2.1253a6, in *Politica*, ed. D. Ross (Oxford: Oxford University Press, 1957); and *The Complete Works of Aristotle*, ed. Barnes, 2: 1986–2129.

55. The pawn is often thought of as a lowly piece, so I refrain from using it as my primary example. But there is an interesting analogy between the pawn and the traditional Crow activity of planting a coup-stick: the pawn will never retreat; it has to be killed instead.

56. M. W. Stirling, *Three Pictographic Autobiographies of Sitting Bull* (Washington, D.C.: Smithsonian Institution, 1938).

57. This is what Aristotle called a "mixed action." He gives the example of people who throw their goods overboard in order to save the ship from sinking; *Nicomachean Ethics* 3.1. The Crow made their decision against a background of dreadful alternatives. They were faced with starvation and with freezing to death. Still, they were able to make a choice and act on it. And that, for Aristotle, is all that is required to make an action voluntary.

58. On Haugeland's interpretation of Heidegger, such a person would

be an exemplar of what, in standard translations, Heidegger called being "authentic" *(eigentlich)*; see "Truth and Finitude."

## II. Ethics at the Horizon

1. Frank B. Linderman, *Pretty-Shield: Medicine Woman of the Crows* (Lincoln: University of Nebraska Press, 1974), p. 8. She spoke those words to Linderman in an interview in 1931.
2. Peter Nabokov, *Two Leggings: The Making of a Crow Warrior* (Lincoln: University of Nebraska Press, 1967), p. 197. See also Nabokov's magisterial *Native American Testimony: A Chronicle of Indian-White Relations from Prophecy to the Present, 1492–2000* (New York: Penguin, 1999).
3. See her excellent discussion in *Reasonably Vicious* (Cambridge, Mass.: Harvard University Press, 2002), pp. 26–52. She draws inspiration from Thomas Aquinas's discussion of practical reason in *Summae Theologiae*, trans. Members of the Dominican Order (New York: McGraw-Hill and Blackfriars, 1963).
4. Indeed, in this initial reservation period mortality rates skyrocketed. Frederick Hoxie reports that although the Crow were constantly at battle during the middle decades of the nineteenth century, the size of their population remained fairly constant. However, nearly one-third of the population recorded in the 1887 census was reported to have died in the next decade: "the Crow people suffered the loss of almost an entire generation of young people at the same time that Agent Armstrong and his successors were launching them on the path to 'civilization'"; Frederick E. Hoxie, *Parading through History: The Making of the Crow Nation in America, 1805–1935* (Cambridge: Cambridge University Press, 1997), p. 133. The increase in the death rate is attributed to living in a confined space with poor sanitary conditions and the introduction of diseases to which they had no resistance. There was a massive outbreak of gastric diseases, in part as a result of the change in diet. Deaths by typhoid, diphtheria, and tuberculosis were com-

mon. This was a monstrous tragedy. But anyone with insight into the human heart must also ask whether one factor in the increased death rate—even among the population infected with disease—was a loss of the will to live.

5. Joseph Medicine Crow, *From the Heart of Crow Country* (1992; reprint, Lincoln: University of Nebraska Press, 2000), pp. 106–107. From this oppression there arose a mordant humor. The author tells us that a new Indian agent arrived on the nearby Cheyenne reservation and announced he was going to get them back on their feet. "The agent did not speak with a forked tongue . . . Within a short time, all the Cheyenne horses were killed off and the Cheyenne were set on foot"; p. 107.

6. After World War II the annual Crow Fair was revived, and it has been increasing in popularity ever since. In recent years the rodeo has become an important component of the fair, and thus horses have been introduced into reservation life for this celebratory competition.

7. See Clifford Geertz, "Thick Description: Toward an Interpretive Theory of Culture," in *The Interpretation of Cultures* (New York: Basic Books, 1973), pp. 3–30. See also Bernard Williams, *Ethics and the Limits of Philosophy* (Cambridge, Mass.: Harvard University Press, 1985), pp. 140–155.

8. Fred W. Voget, *They Call Me Agnes: A Crow Narrative Based on the Life of Agnes Yellowtail Deernose* (Norman: University of Oklahoma Press, 1995), p. 26.

9. Linderman, *Pretty-Shield*, p. 8.

10. See Gabrielle Taylor, *Pride, Shame and Guilt* (Oxford: Clarendon Press, 1984) pp. 53–84; Bernard Williams, *Shame and Necessity* (Berkeley: University of California Press, 1994), pp. 77–102, 212–223; Max Scheler, *On Feeling, Valuing, and Knowing: Selected Writings* (Chicago: University of Chicago Press, 1992); Richard Wollheim, *The Thread of Life* (Cambridge: Cambridge University Press, 1984), pp. 212–221; idem, *On the Emotions* (New Haven: Yale University Press, 1999), pp. 148–220.

11. Alma Hogan Snell, *Grandmother's Grandchild: My Crow Indian Life* (Lincoln: University of Nebraska Press, 2000), p. 42. Snell does report being beaten—but by the principal of her school as punishment for misbehavior. When Pretty Shield found out about it she not only consoled her grandchild; she went to the school with a hatchet and chased a terrified and hollering principal around his desk (p. 98).

12. I have not spent time discussing how practical reason can be deployed in the service of sustaining a pleasure, because even with the transition to reservation life there were still pleasures of eating, drinking, and sex to be had—and prolonged. But it is worth pointing out a degradation that has occurred. Alcoholism has been a terrible problem for the Crow since the beginning of reservation life, and addiction to methamphetamines is now at epidemic levels. See Neela Bearcomesout, "Crank on the Rez," online: http://www.montana.edu/wwwai/imsd/rezmeth/mainpage.htm#_Toc47949091. A person can think about how to sustain these pleasures, so the problem here is not with the deployment of this form of practical reason per se. But this restriction of practical reason does show what terrible ethical and psychological problems can arise when this form of practical reason is deployed in a context that lacks the values and meanings of a stable culture. If all one is thinking about is pleasure, and if the traditional understandings of the useful and the appropriate have collapsed, degradation of some sort is a likely outcome.

13. Plato, *Republic* 2–3, in *Platonis Respublica*, ed. S. R. Slings (Oxford: Oxford University Press, 2003). There are many good English translations, among them *Republic*, trans. G. M. A. Grube, rev. C. D. C. Reeve (Indianapolis: Hackett, 1992); *Republic*, ed. C. D. C. Reeve (Indianapolis: Hackett, 2004); *The Republic*, ed. G. R. F. Ferrari, trans. T. Griffith (Cambridge: Cambridge University Press, 2000). Aristotle, *Nicomachean Ethics* 2.1–4, in *Aristotelis Ethica Nicomachea*, ed. I. Bywater (Oxford: Oxford University

Press, 1980). For recommended translations, see Chapter 1, note 19.

14. Frank B. Linderman, *Plenty-Coups: Chief of the Crows* (Lincoln: University of Nebraska Press, 1962), pp. 11–43; Robert H. Lowie, "From Cradle to Grave," in *The Crow Indians* (Lincoln: University of Nebraska Press, 1983), pp. 33–71.

15. See Martin Heidegger, *Being and Time*, trans. J. Macquarrie and E. Robinson (New York: Harper and Row, 1962), II.3, ¶64, pp. 364–370; and Bernard Williams, "Persons, Character and Morality," in *Moral Luck* (Cambridge: Cambridge University Press, 1981), pp. 1–19. In the psychoanalytic tradition, see Wilfrid Bion, "Attacks on Linking," in *Melanie Klein Today: Developments in Theory and Practice*, ed. E. B. Spillius, vol. 1: *Mainly Theory* (London: Routledge, 1998), pp. 87–101.

16. Linderman, *Plenty-Coups*, p. 59.

17. Lowie, *The Crow Indians*, p. 68.

18. Linderman, *Plenty-Coups*, p. 59.

19. Nabokov, *Two Leggings*, p. 61.

20. Thus Freud has a greater interest in the idea that the wishes themselves might be hidden. But it is not unheard of for a Crow to have a dream in which wishes come to light or get developed. The Crow did not have Jesuit missionaries living among them for centuries as other tribes to the east did. Thus we do not have the same longstanding written record that exists for eastern tribes. As early as 1649, Father Ragueneau, who lived among the Huron, wrote: "In addition to the desires which we generally have that are free, or at least voluntary in us, [and] which arise from previous knowledge of some goodness that we imagine to exist in the thing described, the Hurons believe that our souls have other desires, which are, as it were, inborn and concealed. These, they say, come from the depths of the soul, not through any knowledge, but by means of a certain blind transporting of the soul to certain objects . . . Now they believe that our soul makes these natural desires known to us

by dreams, which are its language." See A. C. Wallace, *The Death and Rebirth of the Seneca* (New York: Vintage, 1972), p. 61. For a detailed account of the theory of dreams see pp. 59–75.

21. See Timothy P. McCleary, *The Stars We Know: Crow Indian Astronomy and Lifeways* (Longrove, Ill.: Waveland, 1997).

22. See, e.g., Phenocia Bauerle, ed., Henry Old Coyote and Barney Old Coyote Jr., comps. and trans., *The Way of the Warrior: Stories of the Crow People* (Lincoln: University of Nebraska Press, 2003), pp. 12, 39, 77, 80.

23. Linderman, *Plenty-Coups*, pp. 63–64.

24. Ibid., pp. 65–67.

25. Ibid., p. 73.

26. Frederick Hoxie says that because the Crow tended to trade with mountain trappers, most Crows in this period had little contact with the white civilization; *Parading through History*, p. 69.

27. Richard White, "The Winning of the West: The Expansion of the Western Sioux in the Eighteenth and Nineteenth Centuries," *Journal of American History* 65 (September 1978), 330.

28. Interestingly, in Freud's secular account of dream-interpretation, he, too, insists that some part of the dream must remain unintelligible. Even though dreams can be interpreted, "There is at least one spot in every dream at which it is unplumbable—a navel as it were, that is its point of contact with the unknown"; Sigmund Freud, *The Interpretation of Dreams*, in *The Standard Edition of the Complete Psychological Works of Sigmund Freud*, ed. and trans. James Strachey, in collaboration with Anna Freud, assisted by Alix Strachey and Alan Tyson, 24 vols. (1953; reprint, London: Hogarth, 1981) (hereafter *SE*), 4: 111n. See also ibid., *SE* 5: 525. For an excellent account of dreams among the Plains Indians, see Lee Irwin, *The Dream Seekers: Native American Visionary Traditions of the Great Plains* (Norman: University of Oklahoma Press, 1994).

29. Medicine Crow gave this account to Robert Lowie at the beginning of the twentieth century; Lowie, *The Crow Indians*, p. 274.

30. Frederick Hoxie, *The Crow* (New York: Chelsea House, 1989), p. 28; cf. Hoxie, *Parading through History*, p. 40.

31. Vigilius Haufniensis (Søren Kierkegaard), *The Concept of Anxiety: A Simple Psychologically Orienting Deliberation on the Dogmatic Issue of Hereditary Sin*, trans. R. Thomte (Princeton: Princeton University Press, 1980); Heidegger, *Being and Time*, especially ¶40, pp. 228–235.

32. Hoxie, *Parading through History*, especially pp. 72–77.

33. I do not presume to pronounce on whether, as Plenty Coups believed, he received spiritual guidance. This account is compatible with either a secular or a religious interpretation. Indeed, the account I am giving is compatible both with Freud's relentlessly secular theory of dreams and with the Crow theory of dreams. In either case one can see this overall process as one of metabolizing the tribe's anxiety. It is just that on the Crow theory they have had spiritual assistance in doing so.

34. See Thomas Kuhn, *The Structure of Scientific Revolutions* (Chicago: University of Chicago Press, 1996). I am indebted to John Haugeland for bringing this analogy to my attention.

35. Linderman, *Plenty-Coups*, p. 67.

36. Idem, *Pretty-Shield*, pp. 87–91.

37. Lowie, *The Crow Indians*, pp. 22–23. To give two gendered examples: (1) A man was derided for clinging to one wife, for always wearing old clothes, for returning from a raid without booty. (2) To a woman one said such things as "You are not good enough to attract any man," "You have never put up a tent," "You have never beaded any blankets," "You have been kidnapped again and again," "You are exceedingly lazy; you never do beadwork or make moccasins for your husband."

38. Joseph Medicine Crow, *From the Heart of Crow Country*, p. 124.

39. As Bernard Williams has put it, "If everything depended on the fear of discovery, the motivations of shame would not be internalized at all. No one would have a character, in effect, and more-

over, the very idea of there being a shame *culture*, a coherent sys-
tem for the regulation of conduct, would be unintelligible";
*Shame and Necessity*, pp. 81–82.

40. Ibid., p. 82.

41. Sigmund Freud, "On Narcissism: An Introduction," in *SE* 14: 73–
102. Richard Wollheim discusses the significance of the ego-ideal
in *The Thread of Life*, pp. 219–224.

42. Sophocles, *Ajax*, trans. J. Moore (Chicago: University of Chicago
Press, 1957), line 690; quoted in Williams, *Shame and Necessity*,
p. 75.

43. Williams, *Shame and Necessity*, pp. 84–85.

44. Ibid., p. 85; quoting from *Ajax* 462 ff.

45. As Plato importantly reminded us, the philosopher is not the person who has wisdom, but the one who knows he lacks it and longs
for it. A *philo-sophos* is a lover of wisdom.

46. Linderman, *Plenty-Coups*, pp. 60 and (2002) 33.

47. Timothy McCleary, "Afterword," in Linderman, *Plenty-Coups*
(2002), p. 174.

48. Though I have not found reference to this in the Crow literature, a
student at the University of Chicago who has worked in Canada
surveying and banding birds tells me that the chickadee has a dual
nature. It is not only an intelligent bird that pays attention to its environment; it is also extremely aggressive. It will fight off and even
kill much larger birds that come into its territory. If Plenty Coups
knew this (and I suspect he did), the chickadee and the eagle
would make a perfect (perhaps uncannily new) match. Thanks to
Moshe Zvi Marvit.

49. Johannes de Silentio (Søren Kierkegaard), *Fear and Trembling: Dialectical Lyric*, ed. and trans. H. V. Hong and E. H. Hong (Princeton: Princeton University Press, 1983), pp. 54–67.

50. Hoxie, *Parading through History*, p. 203.

51. "Native Music Award Thrills Victors," billingsgazette.com, Febru-
ary 17, 2005. Two of their CDs—*It's Time* and *Honest to God*—are
available from Supacrow, Box 357, Crow Agency, MT 59022.

52. Barney Old Coyote, "Crow," in *Encyclopedia of North American Indians*, Houghton Mifflin, online: http://college.hmco.com/history/readerscomp/naind/html/na_009300_crow.htm.

## III. Critique of Abysmal Reasoning

1. Immanuel Kant, *Critique of Pure Reason* A 805 / B 833. There are two good English translations: *Critique of Pure Reason*, ed. and trans. P. Guyer and A. Wood (Cambridge: Cambridge University Press, 1999); and *Critique of Pure Reason*, trans. N. K. Smith (New York: St Martin's, 1965). The question of hope, Kant thinks, is at once practical and theoretical.

2. See Iris Murdoch, *The Sovereignty of Good* (London: Routledge, 1974).

3. See Philip J. Deloria, *Playing Indian* (New Haven: Yale University Press, 1998). And for a devastating account of the political consequences this trope has had, see Vine Deloria, *Custer Died for Your Sins: An Indian Manifesto* (Norman: University of Oklahoma Press, 1988).

4. Frederick E. Hoxie, *Parading through History: The Making of the Crow Nation in America, 1805–1935* (Cambridge: Cambridge University Press, 1997), pp. 148–149.

5. Ibid.

6. Ibid.

7. Ibid., pp. 155–159.

8. One can see remnants of this view in Dee Brown's classic *Bury My Heart at Wounded Knee: An Indian History of the American West* (New York: Henry Holt, 2000), where Crow warriors fighting with U.S. troops against the Sioux are referred to as mercenaries (pp. 289, 307). This account seems more like a Sioux perspective than an "Indian history," as this is certainly not the perspective of the Crows.

9. Aristotle, *Nicomachean Ethics* 2.2.1104a11–30, in *Aristotelis Ethica Nicomachea*, ed. I. Bywater (Oxford: Oxford University Press, 1980). For recommended translations, see Chapter 1, note 19.

10. Ibid., 3.6.1115a–1135.

11. Ibid., 1115a24–30.

12. *Kalon:* noble or beautiful; ibid., 1115a30; b10–15, b20–25; 1116a10–15, b31–32.

13. Ibid., 1117a6–9. I have here basically relied on the translation by Christopher Rowe; however, I have translated *pathos* as "emotion" rather than "affection."

14. Ibid., 1116b5–25.

15. Ibid., 1116b5. See also Plato, *Laches*, in *Complete Works*, ed. J. M. Cooper (Indianapolis: Hackett, 1997), 178a–201c; and *Protagoras* 358d–360e, ibid.

16. Aristotle, *Nicomachean Ethics* 3.6.1117a30–35.

17. Ibid., 1117a9–15, a30–35. The Greek word for "optimism" is *euelpis*.

18. Ibid., 1117a12–14.

19. Sigmund Freud, *The Interpretation of Dreams*, SE 4–5: 1–627.

20. Idem, "Formulations on the Two Principles of Mental Functioning," SE 12: 218–226. I discuss this in *Freud* (New York: Routledge, 2005), chap. 6, "Principles of Mental Functioning," pp. 145–164.

21. See, for instance, Freud, *Beyond the Pleasure Principle*, SE 18: 32–33; "Remarks on the Theory and Practice of Dream-Interpretation," SE 19: 109–121; "Some Additional Notes on Dream-Interpretation as a Whole," SE 19: 127–130; *Inhibitions, Symptoms and Anxiety*, SE 20: 87–174.

22. Freud, *The Ego and the Id*, SE 19: 31, 48; *Group Psychology and the Analysis of the Ego*, SE 18: 105. See also Samuel Ritvo, "Late Adolescence: Developmental and Clinical Considerations," *Psychoanalytic Study of the Child* 26 (1971), 241–263.

23. Plato, *Symposium* 201d–212c, in *Platonis Opera* II, ed. I. Burnet (Oxford: Oxford University Press, 1986). For an English translation see Plato, *Complete Works*, ed. Cooper, pp. 457–505.

24. Plato, *Republic* 6.505e, in *Platonis Respublica*, ed. S. R. Slings (Oxford: Oxford University Press, 2003). For recommended translations, see Chapter 2, note 13. The philosophical significance of this

passage is explored in detail in Robert Adams, *Finite and Infinite Goods: A Framework for Ethics* (Oxford: Oxford University Press, 2002).

25. I explore the Platonic influence on Freud—in particular, how the mature Freud gravitated toward using Eros rather than sexuality as one of his fundamental concepts—in *Love and Its Place in Nature: A Philosophical Interpretation of Freudian Psychoanalysis* (New Haven: Yale University Press, 1999); and in *Freud*, chap. 3, "Sex, Eros and Life," pp. 55–116; "The Introduction of Eros: Reflections on the Work of Hans Loewald," in *Open Minded: Working Out the Logic of the Soul* (Cambridge, Mass.: Harvard University Press, 1998), pp. 123–147; and "Love as a Drive," in *Therapeutic Action: An Earnest Plea for Irony* (New York: Other Press, 2003), pp. 137–178.

26. The expression originated with the psychoanalyst and pediatrician D. W. Winnicott. See, e.g., "Transitional Objects and Transitional Phenomena," in *Playing and Reality* (London: Routledge, 1996), pp. 1–25.

27. Frank B. Linderman, *Plenty-Coups, Chief of the Crows* (Lincoln: University of Nebraska Press, 1962), pp. 33–44.

28. Ibid., pp. 42–43.

29. Should this book attract Crow readers who believe that Plenty Coups did receive a vision from the Little People, they should see that my account of this dream will still apply. But I am writing to show the reader who does not share traditional Crow beliefs that, even so, Plenty Coups's dream played a significant role in his development of courage.

30. See Winnicott, "Transitional Objects and Transitional Phenomena," pp. 1–25.

31. Ibid., pp. 43–44.

32. Linderman, *Plenty-Coups*, p. 47.

33. Ibid., pp. 65–66.

34. This is what Freud would call the manifest content of the dream.

35. Linderman, *Plenty-Coups*, p. 47.

36. Ibid., pp. 38–39.
37. Ibid., p. 65.
38. See Phenocia Bauerle, ed., Henry Old Coyote and Barney Old Coyote Jr., comps. and trans., *The Way of the Warrior: Stories of the Crow People* (Lincoln: University of Nebraska Press, 2003); Joseph Medicine Crow, *From the Heart of Crow Country* (1992; reprint, Lincoln: University of Nebraska Press, 2000), pp. 58–85.
39. Hoxie, *Parading through History*, pp. 80–83, 108–109.
40. See, e.g., Gloria Jahoda, *The Trail of Tears: The Story of the American Indian Removals, 1813–1855* (New York: Random House, 1995); and Merrill D. Beal, *"I Will Fight No More Forever": Chief Joseph and the Nez Perce War* (Seattle: University of Washington Press, 1966).
41. Hoxie, *Parading through History*, pp. 258 ff.
42. Aristotle, *Nicomachean Ethics* 3.1.1110a8–15.
43. Timothy P. McCleary, "Afterword," in Linderman, *Plenty-Coups* (2002), p. 175. The better-known version is a bit sanitized and politically correct: "Education is your most powerful weapon. With education you are the white man's equal; without education you are his victim."
44. Ibid., p. 178.
45. Linderman, *Plenty-Coups*, pp. 227, 228.
46. Ibid., p. 265.
47. McCleary, "Afterword," p. 177.
48. Linderman, *Plenty-Coups*, p. 154.
49. Ibid., p. 78.
50. Ibid., p. 75.
51. Frederic C. Krieg, "Chief Plenty Coups: The Final Dignity," *Montana: The Magazine of Western History* 16 (1966), 37.
52. Ibid., pp. 28–39.
53. See Jean Laplanche, "The Unfinished Copernican Revolution," in *Essays on Otherness* (London: Routledge, 1999), pp. 52–83; and Jonathan Lear, *Happiness, Death, and the Remainder of Life* (Cambridge, Mass.: Harvard University Press, 2000).

54. See James Mooney, *The Ghost-Dance Religion and the Sioux Outbreak of 1890* (Lincoln: University of Nebraska Press, 1991); James Welch and Paul Stekler, *Killing Custer: The Battle of Little Big Horn and the Fate of the Plains Indians* (New York: Penguin, 1995), pp. 267–271; Hoxie, *Parading through History*, pp. 354–355, 362; Brown, *Bury My Heart at Wounded Knee*, pp. 431–442.

55. See Mooney, *The Ghost-Dance Religion*, pp. 821–822.

56. Ibid., p. 847.

57. I am speaking figuratively. There is no historical record that Sitting Bull actually had the vision associated with the Ghost Dance; but he did support the dance and thus those who had had that vision. It is part of the historical record that before the battle of Little Big Horn, he had a vision of men in blue coats falling out of the sky. And he interpreted that to mean success in battle with U.S. soldiers. See Brown, *Bury My Heart at Wounded Knee*, pp. 288–289; Stanley Vestal, *Sitting Bull: Champion of the Sioux* (Norman: University of Oklahoma Press, 1957), pp. 150–151; Welch and Stekler, *Killing Custer*, pp. 50–51. For an extended account of a Sioux warrior's cataclysmic vision see John G. Neihardt, *Black Elk Speaks* (Lincoln: University of Nebraska Press, 1979), especially "The Great Vision," pp. 16–36.

58. See David F. Aberle, *The Peyote Religion among the Navaho* (Norman: University of Oklahoma Press, 1991); Hoxie, *Parading through History*, pp. 220–221, 361. See also Peggy Albright, ed., *Crow Indian Photographer: The Work of Richard Throssel*, with commentaries on the photographs by Crow Tribal Members Barney Old Coyote Jr., Mardell Hogan Plainfeather, and Dean Curtis Bear Claw (Albuquerque: University of New Mexico Press, 1997), p. 216, n. 45.

59. See Fred W. Voget, *The Shoshoni-Crow Sun Dance* (Norman: University of Oklahoma Press, 1984). And see *Yellowtail: Crow Medicine Man and Sun Dance Chief*, as told to Michael Oren Fitzgerald (Norman: University of Oklahoma Press, 1991).

60. McCleary, "Afterword," p. 176. For a similar account see Hoxie, *Parading through History*, p. 345.

61. The author is Barney Old Coyote, a veteran of World War II, who was honored with a Warrior's Homecoming in December 1943. According to his account, that was the second homecoming since World War I.

62. In visiting the Crow Fair—the "tepee capital of the world"—which occurs every year in late August near Crow Agency, Montana, I was struck by one tepee that had the insignia of the U.S. Army emblazoned on an entire side.

# Acknowledgments

I am the beneficiary of a number of extended conversations—stretching out over years—with colleagues at the University of Chicago. With John Haugeland I have been reading and discussing Heidegger, and I have been particularly helped by his interpretation of *Dasein* as a living way of life. With James Conant I have been discussing and teaching Kierkegaard, and my interpretation of subjectivity has grown out of those conversations. With Candace Vogler I have been talking about practical reason and the significance of thick concepts. With Robert Pippin I have been talking about the pressures and meaning of modernity; with Gabriel Lear I have been talking about ethics and the good life; with John Coetzee I have been talking about human blindness, cowardice, and self-deception. I should also like to thank Timothy P. McCleary, who teaches Crow history and culture at Little Big Horn College at Crow Agency, for his unstinting generosity. And discussions with Dr. Samuel Ritvo of the Western New England Institute for Psychoanalysis have helped me understand the crucial role of the ego-ideal in adolescent development. I am also grateful to my friend George Real Bird for showing me how Plenty Coups's ideals are alive among a young generation of Crow. This book could not have been written without their help. The ideas in the book began to take shape when I was preparing to give the Donnellan Lectures at Trinity College Dublin. The ideas developed as I gave talks at the University of Washington at Seattle, the University of New Mexico, St. Olaf College, Columbia University, and the University of Illinois at Champaign–Urbana. I have been helped by many comments and questions, and I am grateful to the faculties and students at all those institutions. I would like specifically to thank Dr. Vasilis Politis of Trinity College Dublin for a question that helped me focus the subject of this book. I also want to thank Anne Gamboa, Administrative Assistant to the Committee on Social Thought, who helps me every day. Thanks, finally, to Phoebe Kosman, Ann Hawthorne, and Lindsay Waters for their insightful and sustained editorial advice. I first heard Plenty Coups's words "After this, nothing happened" about twenty years ago in a paper that was being given by Professor William Cronon. It is only with the passage of time that I recognize that those words lodged within me and never left. This book was motivated in significant part as an attempt to figure out why these words have mattered—and I now realize I have a debt of gratitude to an Indian chief who died at his home on the northwest plains in the shade of some tall trees about a generation before I was born.

# Index

Missouri River, 11, 22

Montana, 1, 5, 11, 26, 32, 74, 124, 135, 137, 144

Moral psychology, 62–66, 104–105

Native American Church, 151

Nazis, 105

Nebraska, 74

No-account dreams, 67

Nomadic way of life, 1, 10–11, 18, 27, 32, 35–36, 41, 55, 57, 59–60, 74–75, 79, 99, 111, 121

North Dakota, 11

No Vitals, 11, 74–75

Oklahoma, 74

Old Coyote, Barney, 99, 178n61

Ontology, 7, 50

Optimism, 113–117

Pan-Indian movement, 151–152

Personal vindication, 142–148

Peyote, 151

Phenomenal happenings, 158n7

Philosophical anthropology, 7

Philosophy, 9

Piegan, 56

Pity, 132–133

Plato, 62, 90, 120–122, 172n45,

175n25; *Phaedrus*, 52; *Republic*, 121

Plenty Coups (Alaxchiiaahush, Many Achievements), 23, 35, 37, 100, 119; photographs of, xii, 54, 102; "After this nothing happened," 1–9, 38, 50–52, 56, 152; in Washington, D.C., 5, 33, 60, 137, 153; on counting coups, 15–16, 19–20, 41; dream-vision of, 20, 66–73, 75–79, 89–92, 97–99, 104, 113–118, 124–136, 147–151, 175n29; as chief, 42–46, 125; shame of, 86–88; reasoning of, 92–96, 100; radical hope of, 103–108, 113–117; and Sitting Bull, 105–108, 148–154; courage of, 110–117, 128, 130–133, 135–136; and historical vindication of the Crow, 136–142; personal vindication of, 142–148; donation of his house, 143–144; name, 147

Plenty Coups State Park, 135, 144

Possibilities, 14, 25, 51, 83–84, 93, 97–99, 141

Poverty, 140

Practical reason, 55–57, 73

Predictions. *See* Dreams

Pretty Eagle, 28, 33

Pretty Shield, 46, 56, 60–62, 80–81, 168n11

Property dreams, 67

Protestant Reformation, 121

*nal of American History* 65 (September 1978), 319–321. Among the valuable work that White cites, see especially W. W. Newcomb Jr., "A Re-Examination of the Causes of Plains Warfare," *American Anthropologist* 52 (1950), 317–330; John C. Ewers, "Intertribal Warfare as the Precursor of Indian-White Warfare on the Northern Great Plains," *Western Historical Quarterly* 6 (1975), 397–410.

25. White, "The Winning of the West," p. 335.

26. Hoxie, *Parading through History*, p. 55. For a traditional Crow story of revenge for a devastation by the Shoshone, see "The Saga of Red Bear," in Bauerle, *The Way of the Warrior*, pp. 39–75.

27. White, "The Winning of the West," pp. 336–337.

28. Hoxie, *Parading through History*, p. 78.

29. Sahlins, *Islands of History*, p. ix. See also Jared Diamond, *Collapse: How Societies Choose or Fail to Succeed* (New York: Viking, 2004).

30. Hoxie, *Parading through History*, p. 141. For a general overview of the loss of Indian lands, see Stuart Banner, *How the Indians Lost Their Land: Law and Power on the Frontier* (Cambridge, Mass.: Harvard University Press, 2005).

31. Cf. Hoxie, *Parading through History*, pp. 154–155; Wagner and Allen, *Blankets and Moccasins*, pp. 243–244.

32. Wagner and Allen, *Blankets and Moccasins*, pp. 243–244.

33. Ibid., p. 247.

34. Hoxie, *Parading through History*, p. 160n.

35. Richard White, *The Middle Ground: Indians, Empires and Republics in the Great Lakes Region, 1650–1815* (Cambridge: Cambridge University Press, 1999), p. x. For a fascinating psychoanalytic discussion of related issues, see D. W. Winnicott, "The Location of Cultural Experience," in *Playing and Reality* (London: Routledge, 1996), pp. 95–103. In the same volume see also "The Place Where We Live," pp. 104–110; and "Transitional Objects and Transitional Phenomena," pp. 1–25.

36. See Hoxie, *Parading through History*, pp. 35–37. And see F. A. Larocque, "Yellowstone Journal," in *Early Fur Trade on the North-*

*ern Plains: Canadian Traders among the Mandan and Hidatsa Indians, 1738–1818*, ed. W. R. Wood and T. D. Thiessen (Norman: University of Oklahoma Press, 1985). For other fascinating nineteenth-century accounts of the Crow, see James Beckworth, *The Life and Adventures of James P. Beckworth* (Lincoln: University of Nebraska Press, 1972); Zenas Leonard, *Narrative of the Adventures of Zenas Leonard* (Lincoln: University of Nebraska Press, 1978); Osborne Russell, *Journal of a Trapper* (Portland: Oregon Historical Society, 1955); Thomas H. Leforge, *Memoirs of a White Crow Indian* (Lincoln: University of Nebraska Press, 1974); George Catlin, *Letters and Notes on the Manners, Customs, and Conditions of the North American Indians* (1857; reprint, New York: Dover, 1973).

37. Wagner and Allen, *Blankets and Moccasins*, p. 240.

38. On the reservation today he is known as Wraps His Tail, and thus I so refer to him.

39. See Cora Diamond's marvelous essay, "Losing Your Concepts," *Ethics*, 1988; as well as Alasdair MacIntyre, *After Virtue* (Notre Dame: University of Notre Dame Press, 1981); and G. E. M. Anscombe, "Modern Moral Philosophy," *Philosophy* 33 (1958), reprinted in *The Collected Papers of G. E. M. Anscombe*, vol. 3: *Ethics, Religion and Politics* (Oxford: Blackwell, 1983), pp. 26–42.

40. John Haugeland is working out an interpretation of Heidegger's *Being and Time* in which *Dasein* is understood not in terms of an individual human being and his or her capacities, but rather in terms of a *living way of life*. The death of *Dasein* is thus the collapse of that way of life, and being-towards-death is the way we relate to that possibility of collapse. See his *Heidegger Disclosed* (forthcoming). How this works as an interpretation of Heidegger— is Haugedegger Heidegger?—is Haugeland's task. But this interpretation is of enormous help in conceptualizing the challenges Plenty Coups had to face. In particular, students of Heidegger can read this essay as an inquiry into being-towards-death: Plenty Coups's way of comporting himself in relation to the death of *Dasein*. See also Haugeland, "Truth and Finitude: Heidegger's

Transcendental Existentialism," in *Heidegger, Authenticity, and Modernity: Essays in Honor of Hubert L. Dreyfus*, ed. M. A. Wrathall and J. Malpas, vol. 1 (Cambridge, Mass.: MIT Press, 2000), pp. 43–77. The idea that concepts—and the acts that instantiate them—have life only within the context of a form of life is most clearly associated with the later work of Wittgenstein. See G. E. M. Anscombe and R. Rhees, eds., G. E. M. Anscombe, trans., *Philosophical Investigations* (Oxford: Blackwell, 1978). And see John Rawls, "Two Conceptions of Rules," *Philosophical Review* 64 (1955), 3–13.

41. Hoxie, *Parading through History*, p. 345. See also the contemporary accounts in *New York Times*, November 12, 1921; and *Chicago Tribune*, November 12, 1921. And see John C. Ewers, "A Crow Chief's Tribute to the Unknown Soldier," *American West* 8 (1971), 30–35.

42. When I have presented these ideas in lectures, I have regularly been asked about similarities to the Jewish holocaust in World War II. Crow concepts could, I think, have survived their own holocaust. A more relevant analogy therefore seems to be the destruction of the Temple. With that destruction certain traditional forms of orientation—e.g., toward a priestly caste, toward the Temple, toward sacrifice—became impossible. There were no longer viable ways of so orienting oneself. Unlike the Crow, the Jews had their Book; and the rabbis were able to use it to construct a liturgy that would be specifically applicable in conditions of exile and diaspora. In this context, Plenty Coups's decision to tell his story to a white man so that it might be written down and preserved as a traditional story takes on added significance.

43. Fred W. Voget, *The Shoshoni-Crow Sun Dance* (Norman: University of Oklahoma Press, 1984); Michael O. Fitzgerald, *Yellowtail: Crow Medicine Man and Sun Dance Chief* (Norman: University of Oklahoma Press, 1991). And see Dale K. McGinnis and Floyd W. Sharrock, *The Crow People* (Phoenix: Indian Tribal Series 1972) p. 68.

44. It is a striking fact that the dance that was invented on the Indian reservations and soon passed to the Crow tribe is the Ghost Dance. See Hoxie, *Parading through History*, pp. 354–362. This is a dance expressing hope and confidence in the coming of an Indian messiah and the restoration of buffalo and their traditional way of life. White people would be destroyed in an apocalypse, and the ghosts of their Indian ancestors would return to their traditional lives. I discuss the Ghost Dance in the final chapter. See also J. Mooney, *The Ghost-Dance Religion and the Sioux Outbreak of 1890* (Lincoln: University of Nebraska Press, 1991).

45. Of course, it is a euphemism to say that the buffalo "went away": they were destroyed. Even Plenty Coups—as honest as he was— seems to have swerved from a simple statement of this brutal truth.

46. See Michael Thompson, *Life and Action* (forthcoming); and G. E. M. Anscombe, *Intention* (Cambridge, Mass.: Harvard University Press, 2000).

47. See M. Heidegger, *The Basic Problems of Phenomenology*, trans. Albert Hofstadter (Bloomington: Indiana University Press, 1988), pp. 229–274.

48. Aristotle, *Physics* 4.10–14, in *Aristotelis Physica*, ed. D. Ross (Oxford: Oxford University Press, 1951). For an English translation see *The Complete Works of Aristotle*, ed. Barnes, 1: 315–446. I discuss Aristotle's theory of time in *Aristotle: The Desire to Understand* (Cambridge: Cambridge University Press, 1988), pp. 74–83. For an excellent account of Aristotle's theory of time, see Ursula Coope, *Time for Aristotle* (Oxford: Oxford University Press, 2005).

49. See K. A. Appiah, *The Ethics of Identity* (Princeton: Princeton University Press, 2004).

50. The inspiration for this conception of subjectivity comes from Søren Kierkegaard's pseudonymously published text, Johannes Climacus, *Concluding Unscientific Postscript to the Philosophical Fragments: A Mimic-Pathetic-Dialectic Composition: An Existential Contribution*. There are two translations, both recommended: